Dawn, Dusk and

DEER

Dawn, Dusk and
DEER

BY

ARTHUR CADMAN, OBE

Illustrations by
C. F. TUNNICLIFFE

•THE•
SPORTSMAN'S
PRESS
LONDON

This edition published in 1989 by The Sportsman's Press
© Arthur Cadman 1989
First published 1966

TO THE KEEPERS OF THE NEW FOREST
WHO HAVE TAUGHT ME SO MUCH

British Library Cataloguing in Publication Data
Cadman, Arthur
    Dawn, dusk and deer
    1. Deer
    I. Title
    599'.73'57
    ISBN 0–948253–41–X

Printed and bound in Great Britain at
Bookcraft (Bath) Ltd

Contents

Foreword by
THE LORD DULVERTON,
CBE, TD, MA, DL

*Former President of The British Deer Society and
The Red Deer Commission*

I am so glad that its author has decided to embark on a new publication of *Dawn, Dusk and Deer*. To all who have a love of the countryside and its wild creatures, and especially if not exclusively the deer, it is a true box of delights. I first met Arthur a good many years ago, down in the New Forest, and was fascinated by his deep knowledge of the Roe and Fallow there, and his system of managing them, in which he was one of the early pioneers, at a time when this was usually far too haphazard.

Arthur's patient fieldcraft and alert observation of all wildlife shines through his pages, embellished as they are by the art of Charles Tunnicliffe.

After retiring as Deputy Surveyor of the New Forest, he betook himself to the lovely wilds of the Highlands where, besides pursuing his early love of wild-fowling in the Firths of Moray and Dornoch, he managed the Roe deer stalking on the famous Novar estate for eleven years, and has continued to stalk Red, Fallow, Roe and Sika deer 'from Ross-shire to Cornwall'.

Now 'retired' to Norfolk, what a wealth of experiences he has to draw upon, what tales to tell, what insights into the lives of the wild. As I said before – a box of delights is about to be renewed.

Introduction

Since this book was written, nearly 25 years ago, there has been great progress in the deer world. Legislation covering close seasons and permitted weapons is now adequate. Equally important is the improved and more widespread knowledge of proper control, of good management, of deer behaviour and of deer populations. There are many good technical books of reference available today.

At the same time, problems remain, deer continue to spread. In many cases the increase in numbers and the disproportionate balance between the sexes give rise for concern. In particular the enormous increase of Red deer numbers in the Scottish Highlands, with a shortage of mature stags, needs urgent attention, especially as the wintering ground has diminished. Elsewhere Roe are still spreading and Muntjac have colonised many new areas.

There is more commercial stalking which is of benefit to the finances of estates.

One great advance is the advent of *Stalking*, a monthly magazine devoted to deer. There is much expertise in its pages.

Arthur Cadman
April 1989

The Roe Buck

A shadow in the shadows
So motionless he stood,
Both unconcerned, yet watchful,
From deep within the wood.

His nostrils twitching slightly
While testing out the breeze;
His soft eyes watching brightly
For movement through the trees.

Still, waiting like a statue,
For him all time was made.
Then daintily and softly
He stepped into the glade.

With pricked ears list'ning keenly
To catch the lightest sound
And russet coat, groomed cleanly,
Matching the fern, long-browned.

His antlers caught the sunlight
As he frayed a sapling tree,
And left its stem a cream-white
For the foresters to see.

He plucked a leafy bramble
And then moved slowly on.
A branch shook ten yards further –
I knew that he was gone.

I

The First Day of Summer

The May Day celebration was once a peaceful effusion of joy to welcome the warmth of the sun on the first day of summer. The maypole meant laughter and dancing and the crowning of a May Queen. Today all that has gone, yet to a countryman the first of May still means what it was meant to mean even before the first maypole. It signifies the bursting of myriads of green buds, the uncurling of fern fronds, the sight of the first blue-bells and the first swifts; the quick wings of a turtle dove and the call of the cuckoo ringing clear above the dawn chorus. It is the time for the renewal of all life.

One May Day, in the heart of a forest in England, it was dark under the trees, but towards the east the night sky was a shade lighter, and it was just possible to make out the fine tracery of the upper branches. A pipistrelle bat wavered jerkily around the tree tops as he hunted for moths. The air was full of the melodious notes of a cock blackbird, who had no doubt at all that the first moments of summer were coming.

By the fence of a plantation of conifers the faint shadow of a man moved silently along the ditch. A soft wind whispered through the trees and brought to his nose the earthy smell of damp humus. Far away a tawny owl hooted.

Near the gate of the plantation, the man, still almost invisible, left the ditch and stepped on to a deer path. This he followed, moving very quietly and slowly, until he came to a huge oak tree: a tree which had been growing there for three hundred years. A crude ladder led up to a large fork in the tree. Swiftly he climbed the ladder and settled himself upon his bag which he placed on a wide board, nailed across the fork. This provided a solid seat. There he sat motionless, his face concealed by a green mask, a pair of powerful field-glasses hanging around his neck.

The seat looked out over a wide grassy glade where the first bluebells were just showing. The glade was fringed with giant oak trees and beyond was an area of newly-planted small firs within the fence of the plantation. Out to the right a shallow valley fell away into the distance. The valley was framed with birch trees, and a thin silver corkscrew marked the course of a tiny stream, its banks golden with kingcups.

To the east the sky took on a salmon glow. A wood pigeon began to coo: 'Take two cows, Taffy, take two cows, Taffy'.

The man sitting on the seat thought: 'Surprising how early the odd pigeon starts to coo. As a boy I always used to think pigeons only cooed when the sun was up.'

The light became good enough to scan the young plantation with field-glasses. He sat relaxed, enjoying the beauty of the morning. A Roe buck had been doing serious damage in the plantation, and he had got up at 4.15 a.m. to find out what was happening and to see what the buck was like.

Now the whole sky was turning scarlet; a moment later the red rim of the sun peeped over the horizon, and the colour of the early morning sky began to fade. Nature's moods are often fickle and frequent change is usual. Animals are well aware of these changes in advance; it is part of their life. Man, being less sensitive, is able to read only the more obvious signs, such as a flaming sunrise. So one thing was certain – by three o'clock in the afternoon it would be raining.

Slowly he slid a hand into his pocket and pulled out an apple. He studied every inch of the ground near the oak tree to satisfy himself that no deer was nearby, and then took a bite. A Roe buck has such an acute sense of hearing that he will hear a man bite a crisp apple or the faint rustle of the strap of a camera against a tweed jacket. He may not

be alarmed, but he will be alerted by such sounds, while any metallic sound will send him bounding away into cover.

Having finished eating the apple he let the core fall. It bounced off a large limb and fell to the ground about eight feet from the base of the ladder.

His eyes were continually searching the area through his glasses. He saw a wren fly into some ivy thinly struggling up the bole of another oak tree, some forty yards away. He could just make out the edge of its nest. Since the severe 1962–63 winter the wren had become a rare bird.

In the middle of the area of young Douglas fir, a slight movement caught his eye. His glasses swung round to focus on the spot. The ear of a Roe doe flicked again and at once he could make out her outline, lying in a patch of dead bracken. A moment later she stood up, stretched herself, and scratched behind her right ear with her right hind foot.

Then she plucked a half uncurled leaf of bramble and chewed it slowly. She wandered across the area plucking a leaf here and there, pausing to take a few bites from a patch of fresh green grass. When she had moved about twenty yards, the man suddenly became aware of another deer. It was a yearling kid. To be precise she was three weeks less than a year old because she had been born in the third week of the previous May. By now she was only a little smaller than her mother. The yearling was more frolicsome than the old doe. She would suddenly move off a few yards to investigate something that had caught her eye. But when grazing, she would not lift her head until she had eaten most of what held her attention. This lack of alertness in young Roe deer is most marked and has cost many a youngster its life.

Normally Roe deer have twins, in contrast to other species of British deer which very rarely bear twins. But Roe kids are very vulnerable to foxes and dogs. The doe may protect one kid when she cannot protect both. When a Roe doe is seen with only one kid it may be assumed that most probably she has had twins but has lost one of them.

The two deer fed slowly towards the fence. When they reached it they both slipped into the ditch and then squeezed under the lowest strand of wire as smoothly and silently as two shadows. They wandered here and there, apparently at random, but still maintaining a general direction towards the old oak tree. Soon they were only twenty yards away. The glasses were hardly needed to see the loose tufts of their old winter coats, with here and there a small patch of rich red summer coat showing through, especially on the lower part of the neck.

The yearling walked directly towards the base of the ladder. Suddenly she spotted the apple core. She stopped and raised her left foreleg, pointing her bent knee towards the apple core. Her neck and head were stretched out to their fullest extent. No pointer working the heather in August ever made a better point! She remained motionless for fully thirty seconds. Then she advanced slowly, lowered her head, picked up and ate the apple core.

The man sitting silently in the oak tree was dumbfounded. Why had she not smelled the hated human scent? Perhaps a man's teeth have less scent than an apple! Then he remembered another incident he had witnessed the year before. He had sat for two hours in a high seat and had not seen a deer at all – although he had watched a vixen and, later, two water shrews playing around the base of the tree. Three stems of sweet chestnut growing from a stool had irritated him for they obscured his view of an open space. At last he had come down off the seat, and having a folding saw with him, had cut down and removed two of the stems. He ran his left hand up the third to take a grip in readiness for sawing it through. Then he had changed his mind and let it go. It would grow into a tree one day and the other two bushier stems had really been the cause of the trouble.

He had collected his rifle, bag and glasses and was walking back to the car when he saw a Roe heading for the area where the seat was. It was moving through thick undergrowth and he was quite unable to discern whether it was the buck he wanted or, even, whether it was a buck at all. So he had returned very quietly to the seat and had not been there many moments before a Roe doe stepped into the glade which was overlooked by the seat. She walked straight up to the chestnut stump and ran her nose up and down the stem where his own left hand had been but a few moments before. Then she licked the freshly cut surface from which one of the two sawn-off branches had been cut. After that she had gone quietly on her way!

Meanwhile, the two does wandered past the great oak tree and disappeared among the holly bushes beyond.

A cuckoo flew with shivering wings across the glade towards the oak. It settled on a branch fifteen feet above the man's head and started to call. Then it caught sight of him and was away through the green foliage in a flash of blue-grey plumage, uttering a single startled 'Woch.'

Two minutes later, from behind a snowy white blackthorn bush by the little stream where the kingcups shone golden in the morning sun, a Roe buck stepped out. He stood there, head held high, yet quite motionless, while he surveyed the glade.

The man's glasses were focused upon the Roe's head. The six-point antlers were well above his ears, the brow tines being well formed. As he stood there in a shaft of morning sunlight, broadside on, he offered a perfect killing shot. But the rifle remained across the man's knees. The Roe's antlers were still in velvet, and the man knew that he was not the one which had been doing the damage. In fact he was a fine young buck, and he did not even belong to that part of the forest. He was passing through looking for a territory which was not occupied by a stronger buck.

With his forefoot the young buck made a small scrape on the ground beside the slender stem of a young alder buckthorn. Then, very gently, he rubbed his antlers up and down the stem. He was testing the state of the velvet which protected his antlers. Evidently it was not yet ready, for he passed on, without so much as scraping a half-inch length of bark off the sapling alder buckthorn.

The Roe buck walked across the centre of the glade. He was well fed and did not pause to nibble the young bramble shoots. He dropped into the drain and passed under the plantation fence at the same point that the doe and yearling had used on their way out. Once inside he turned along the fence and entered a thicket of older trees, where he was hidden.

The man in the oak tree knew that it was time for him to go back, but he lingered in order to enjoy the beauty of the morning for a little while longer. He would not have exchanged the last two hours for anything.

Many hundreds of thousands of people can never know what a May morning in a forest is like, because their path of life leads in a different direction: via the bus, the tube and the pavement.

So the idea of writing a simple book about deer came out of this May morning – a book about their habits and paths, and the many incidents which may be experienced while watching them.

In this age of rush and turmoil, of journeys made through space, of computers and problems which are beyond the power of any one man's brain, how pleasant it is to follow the advice carved upon a seat in a lonely part of the New Forest:

'Sit still, look long and hold yourself quiet.'

How few people have the ability to do this simple thing! A tramp once said to me how much better the world would be if those who govern and hold power in their hands – politicians, directors, generals, business tycoons – were made to do just this for one whole hour, alone in the heart of the country, on one day each week of their lives!

II

'Sit Still, Look Long and Hold Yourself Quiet'

That is the best possible advice to give to any young naturalist, but it is far from easy to accomplish. A considerable amount of self-discipline has to be practised before one can sit still without fidgeting.

To hold oneself quiet is easier when alone than in company, but even then complete stillness is difficult. A deer will hear the slightest movement; and a deer has greater patience than a man. For instance, you see a deer run behind a bush or other natural cover, so you freeze instantly. The moments pass. A fly settles on your nose. You manage to blow it off, resisting the impulse to raise a hand. More moments slide away, and more flies, gnats, midges and mosquitoes arrive. At long last you relax. The deer must have moved on, you think, so you brush off that insistent mosquito. Still no sign of the deer. So you decide to proceed on your way and take a step forward – and the deer bounds away. It had been motionless, watching you all the time.

But the rewards for those who can train themselves to sit still and hold themselves quiet are great. (To this end a good insect repellent is a valuable aid!) Often some creature that was quite unexpected will appear.

Of all creatures the jay is the most likely to spot you. He is not often fooled unless he happens to land on a branch very close to you. Then there will be a moment while he scans the distance and he may miss a more obvious object beside him. But in a few seconds he will see you and then for a split second he may be too surprised to screech. But this rarely happens.

Next to the jay an old cock pheasant is the wiliest creature. He misses very little. Being used to keeping one eye on the sky, presumably on the lookout for hawks, he will not often miss you however still you may sit on a deer seat. Deer are not afraid of hawks, and it is because they keep a constant lookout for danger at ground level that they fail to look upwards to a deer seat.

Grey squirrels are also quick to notice movement, but they readily accept a motionless human being in a tree. I have had one come and sit on the seat beside me within a few inches of my body. When he finally saw me he leapt several feet – and then crept back round the branch because he could not believe that he really had been sitting next to a man. After that he raced down the trunk and disappeared all in a second. Squirrels are the noisiest animals in the forest – other than man, of course. If you hear a creature rustling through the undergrowth behind, you need not turn round to see if it is a deer: it is sure to be a squirrel. You may just hear a deer, but more often they arrive without a sound and fade away again in silence.

Because squirrels are such active creatures it is entertaining to watch them, even though it is annoying to find out just how many of these pests there are. Squirrels chasing each other give a delightful display of agility. They race up and down trunks and seem to fly through the branches even on to the most slender twigs, making prodigious leaps between. A squirrel gathering oak leaves for its nest or drey will bring them a considerable distance – some thirty or forty yards. The leaves are held in a round ball in its mouth and the journey is done on the ground to the foot of the tree where its nest is. After running up the bole and depositing the leaves in its nest, as likely as not the squirrel will go off in a different direction and forget all about the nest. The most irritating squirrel is the one that spots some movement and starts chattering at you. It will go on and on – and on. When it has worked itself up into a nattering, chattering rage it is not easily frightened. You

can wave your handkerchief at it, throw your hat in the air or even jump up and down on your seat – actions which will send a normal squirrel scurrying away. But the scolding squirrel will just continue to scold – louder than ever.

A mouse makes more noise than an elephant as it rustles through dead leaves. Once I watched two water shrews playing below my seat. They are rare creatures with dark, almost black, fur, but the hairs under the tail are white.

Hares and rabbits are not entirely silent in their movements, and they are noisy if they wish to give the alarm. Badgers are noisy creatures, as they do not seem to care who hears them. When they sit down and scratch they make a proper job of it.

But a fox will glide past in complete silence, stopping frequently to listen and look and test the wind. Incidentally, a dog fox will cock his leg nearly as frequently as a dog; when tracking in the snow it is not long before this tell-tale sign betrays his sex. Not long ago our game warden saw a dog fox cock his leg against the wheel of the head keeper's Land-Rover – a piece of vulpine impertinence!

Once, sitting at dusk on a deer seat, I watched a vixen and her four cubs coming down the ride towards me. She lay down right under the seat and suckled her young.

Wood pigeons, though very quick to spot movement, do not readily see a motionless man sitting in a tree. But the wild life of the forest pays a good deal of attention to the movements of pigeons. A pigeon settling in a tree with a loud clatter is a sign that all is well. But three or four pigeons bursting out of a tree when disturbed will alarm deer for quite a distance. This is a serious factor which has to be taken into consideration when stalking through a wood.

On summer evenings, while waiting for a Roe buck, a most pleasing sight is a roding woodcock. You hear his queer chuntering grunt shortly before he appears. Then, as he comes over on short stiff wing beats, you may hear a tiny squeak, an altogether inadequate noise. He will circle away over the tree tops, but soon he will be back again, sometimes accompanied by another male. Roding – the old name for the evening flight – goes on from February until about midsummer's day, and then one realises that the woodcock are roding no more.

Nightjars continue their 'churring' serenade long after midsummer and the sound never fails to thrill me. Often the male, who has two distinctive spots on his wings, will clap his wings for good measure.

The dawn chorus in May is an experience not to be missed. To sit still among the first soft green leaves of spring, while every bird within reach pours forth his song to greet the rising sun, is a supreme joy.

As a contrast, go abroad through the forest when an autumn gale tears at the trees. The wind whines and moans through the branches, great limbs creak and groan, leaves whirl through the air and rain falls steadily. Then you will find that forest creatures take but little notice of man. They have to compete with greater forces. Many common animals, including Roe buck and rabbit, just disappear. Others remain cowering where they can find refuge, or battle against the wind, striving to reach their known place of shelter. Under these conditions it is possible to walk right up to Fallow deer, provided one watches the wind. To be out under such conditions is exhilarating.

One May morning I was watching about forty Fallow deer on a re-seeded area. Some were feeding and some lying down, the nearest deer being an old doe lying down. She was slightly suspicious, no doubt having seen some movement.

Presently a jackdaw settled on her head and started to pick ticks from behind her ears. She took not the slightest notice of the bird and continued to stare towards the place where I was. Then a second jackdaw joined the first. One perched between her ears and the other settled on her left ear. The weight of the bird depressed the deer's ear and when the bird hopped on to the deer's neck, its ear flipped back into a normal position. But apart from that the doe made no movement and still took no notice. She never shook her head nor even glanced at the jackdaw, which flew away after about three minutes of feasting on ticks! Starlings and magpies sometimes settle on deer, too.

One evening in August I was moving slowly along a ride looking for a Roe buck when I came upon a magnificent Fallow buck. He was standing broadside on, about forty yards away. Some object I could not see, because it was round the corner, held his attention. As I stood watching him a robin flew up and settled on his right antler, which was still in velvet, though fully formed. The buck took not the slightest notice. Four times the robin flew down to the ground to pick up a grub, and returned each time to one or other of the great buck's antlers. Not once did he so much as shake his head. Presently he stepped into the undergrowth and disappeared. The robin remained, perched on a hazel bough. Though I went right up to the corner I never found what it was that had held the buck's attention.

The following winter (1962–63) was one of unprecedented harshness. I had undertaken to procure a good Fallow buck for the Glasgow museum and I had selected a buck with a 'bumble' foot that frequented the area where I had seen the robin and the buck in August. There was a foot of snow on the ground frozen as hard as concrete. Already many wild creatures had succumbed to the biting cold and starvation. Before dawn, muffled up to the ears, I climbed into a deer seat and waited. It was bitterly cold and my breath froze on my face mask. As it got light I could see dark patches on the snow where the deer had pawed through to the ground and scattered brown oak leaves on the surface while searching for acorns. But that had been before the snow had been frozen too hard for them to scrape it away. Now the forest was dead in a dreary and deserted whiteness. Neither bird nor animal moved and the cold bit into my bones. Then I heard a slight rustle. A robin was turning over the leaves disturbed by the deer. Presently it flew up and with a flick of wings settled on the muzzle of my rifle. Then it flitted nearer and settled on the breech of the rifle between my hands. Altogether it settled four times on my rifle! Seldom have I felt so helpless, for I had not the tiniest crumb of food to offer this starving feathered mite, so trusting in its extreme need. I would like to think that it did survive. It was probably the same robin that had alighted on the buck's antlers in August, for that had only been a hundred yards away, but it is doubtful if it lived. The wrens had already died and so had many hedge sparrows, song thrushes, Dartford warblers and stonechats. Woodpeckers had been hard hit, too, and under the holly bushes lay the wasted corpses of wood pigeons and woodcock. The robin was the only living thing I saw that morning.

The story of the Glasgow buck is of interest. Before I knew he had a 'bumble' foot I had seen him standing in the snow and decided that I would not shoot him. Then the keeper reported a very lame buck and his description tallied with the buck I had seen and not shot. It took me two more outings before I found him again. I recognised him at once, but in deep snow it is not easy to obtain a good view of a deer's foot. It was some time before I was quite certain that he was the lame buck. At last I was able to see his injured foot – it was swollen to twice the normal size. It was necessary to shoot him without damaging the hide, as a high velocity bullet makes an ugly gash when it emerges from a broadside shot. The buck solved the problem by turning and facing me. The bullet made a tiny hole in the front of his neck and there was no other external damage.

The Museum authorities wanted the whole beast and they had agreed to pay all expenses connected with the transaction. The internal organs were carefully removed through a very small slit. Then the inside was packed with salt and the whole animal very carefully wrapped up in layers of straw and hessian. To make it easy for the railwaymen to transport it two poles were lashed to the bundle so that it could be carried like a stretcher. Two keepers took all morning to do this and they were very glad to hand it over to Southampton station for consignment to Glasgow. But two hours later the buck was back in the forest. A railway official had discovered some regulation which permitted bodies to be consigned by rail only if they were in lead containers! So the buck had to be unpacked, skinned out and careful measurements taken of all its dimensions so as to help the Scottish taxidermists. Everyone was thoroughly fed up with the whole operation by the time it was finished. It was particularly annoying because whole stags are frequently consigned by rail from Scotland to destinations in England.

After the snow had gone I was sitting on a deer seat on a private estate where I had undertaken to help to control some Sika deer. I looked out over a broad clearing. Many pigeons came to roost in the plantation behind me, until I estimated that there were fifty within thirty yards. Then two cock pheasants, one an old English blackneck and the other a normal type of ringneck with no pure blood in his make-up, faced up to each other not many yards from my seat. They crouched beak to beak, tails stretched out behind. But the blackneck, suddenly thinking discretion better than valour, turned and took to his wings. He passed so close to me that I could feel the air disturbance of his wing-beats. The other puffed himself up and began to strut away full of masculine pride. Then, out of the corner of his eye, he saw me. His surprise was enormous and he quickly skulked away, belly close to the ground.

A few moments later my attention was drawn to a movement opposite, as a gorgeous cock Amherst pheasant came running jerkily out of the cover. He was joined by three more. They flirted their long silver tails and made play by running at each other, resplendent in their glorious colours. Actually none of the four was pure Amherst as they all had some Golden pheasant blood in them, made evident by the scarlet hues in their plumage. It is rare indeed to see such a brilliant display by four males in the wild state. And it more than made up for the complete absence of deer that evening. When I moved to descend from my seat all fifty pigeons clattered away in dire alarm.

An experienced deer man knows that if he has to move he must make all his movements with studied slowness. The novice is always hurrying forward to see what is around the next corner. The expert takes ages to move a few yards, and even then he may never see what is round the next bend. But he sees far more before he ever reaches it.

One day I was stalking a Roe buck. He was feeding away from me in fairly open woodland, and I could move only when his head was down.

Of necessity progress was slow. Between myself and the buck a fox came out on to the ride, paused and then went on his way. I was half way to where the fox had appeared when a woodcock came flying down the ride to settle almost exactly where the fox had been. It then fluttered up and down twice. I guessed that the fox had disturbed its brood and that it was now collecting them. When at last I reached the same place I was keeping one eye very much on the look-out for the woodcock. Suddenly she flushed not two yards from me. I saw quite clearly a young woodcock held between her thighs. Her flight was heavy, like that of a hawk carrying prey. I have now seen this rare event ten times altogether.

One October morning I had stalked to within range of a Fallow buck. I was crouching motionless behind a beech tree, waiting for the buck to turn and present a certain shot. A wild gale was blowing and the tops of the trees were bent over, the branches straining away from the trunks. The buck turned and I raised the rifle and slid the sights up the inside of his front leg until they were steady on his heart. Such a moment demands complete concentration and one is oblivious to all

26

else. Yet at that very moment a sound impinged upon my mind and my attention wavered. For a moment I could not place the sound, half dispersed by the wind. It was no woodland sound. Then I realised that I was hearing the wild clamour of geese! I looked up and there they were, some thirty whitefronts, beating purposefully into the teeth of the gale, their great pinions almost brushing the tops of the trees. I watched spellbound – the first geese of winter. When they had passed I remembered the buck. He had moved and my chance was gone, but it didn't matter anyway, because my heart was away up on the Solway with the tide racing and the pinkfeet battling against the south-west gale.

But there are many things besides deer and other animals for him who 'looks long'. The first brimstone butterfly is a sure sign of warmer spring days. Once, on the bark of an oak tree beside the seat on which I was sitting, I spotted a red underwing moth. Its mottled grey upper wings exactly matched the colour of oak bark, and I had been looking at it for some time before I saw it. On the other hand the green emerald moth is there for all to see – a thing of great beauty.

Ants often appear forty feet or more from the ground. Where you find one you usually find more. They have their main runs or paths, just like deer and other animals, and these paths may run over land for considerable distances or follow precise routes up tree trunks and along branches. If one of these ant paths happens to cross the branch on which one's arms or feet rest, it is wise to give them right of way!

One evening I was waiting motionless beside a small forest pool. The light was fading and I was about to leave, when a small bird topped the trees and then dropped like a stone towards the pool. I was only half aware of it until I heard a distinct splash. What bird only a quarter of the size of a teal would do that? Three more splashes followed in quick succession as the bird seemed to throw itself at the surface of the pool. Then there was a blue flash and I found myself looking at a kingfisher perched on a branch not many yards away.

A sight which most stalkers remember is that of dew on spiders' webs in September. The first rays of the sun catching the dew-drops lights the webs with a myriad sparkling pinpoints. Intriguing patterns are everywhere and often there is not a square yard without its gossamer. An hour later the dew has evaporated and the countless webs become invisible.

One of the most beautiful things in all nature is a Roe kid. When sitting quietly on a deer seat one June evening I watched a Roe doe sauntering through the forest. By then all does should have dropped their kids, and so I wondered if she was barren. She wandered through the forest apparently without a care in the world. Here, she plucked a bramble shoot, and there a sweet chestnut leaf, rolling it into her mouth from the tip, and not pulling it from its stem until the whole large leaf was in her mouth. She took some time, perhaps twenty minutes, to reach the seat. There she stood, immediately below me, looking intently across the glade. Suddenly she made a curious whicker, rather like the call of a young tawny owl. Immediately a brown creature rushed at her from the undergrowth some twenty yards away. It was her kid, a beautiful, dainty, dappled creature only a little larger than a hare. The doe suckled her kid within a few yards of me and then they went on their way, the kid gambolling and running playfully hither and thither.

Often, when one is still and silent, most unexpected incidents crop up. On one occasion, when waiting silently to watch fox cubs at their earth, a youth sauntered past with a gun under his arm. I had to give up my vigil to ask him whether or not he had a permit to carry a gun in the forest. I was surprised when he told me that he had, because I knew that I had not issued a permit to him; but his permit turned out to be merely a gun licence taken out that day. I explained that that did not give him the right to carry a gun in the forest.

However, he insisted rather truculently that he had the right to shoot anywhere, so I had no alternative but to offer him the opportunity to prove this at the local police station. When I opened my car door to let him in, he took off at high speed down the gravel road. There are few things I dislike more than running, and nowadays my figure is not exactly suited to this form of exercise. Nevertheless, I took off after him, pounding along as best I could, without much hope of catching him. I was tying to think of suitable words to stop him in his tracks, but I had no spare breath left for shouting! Such is the power of guilt that the sound of my pounding footsteps made the lad panic, and with a sudden swerve he dived into the undergrowth. Had he remained on the road he might have got clean away. But in the undergrowth I knew every bush and deer track, and I could crash through the bushes while he had to run round. When I finally caught up with him I was purple in the face, and it was some time before I regained enough breath to speak my mind.

It was his unlucky day, because he had bought the gun only that morning, and I heard later that he got into severe trouble with his uncle with whom he was staying!

Another lad whom I found with a ·410 in the forest was on leave from the Merchant Navy. He, too, thought that a gun licence entitled him to shoot in the forest, and he challenged me to take him to the police station to prove this. He was a polite lad and I could not help smiling as he held open each gate in turn for me to drive through! At the police station he was sadly disillusioned about his right to carry a gun in the forest.

Irresponsible youths with guns do a great deal of damage, and cause much suffering to animals and birds because they pay no regard to close seasons and often only wound, for they are generally poor shots. They are also a grave danger to fellow human beings because they have very little idea of safety.

On one occasion eight keepers were on a vermin shoot. They surrounded a small area of scrub and much to their surprise found a poacher with a gun cowering in the middle. He thought they had turned out a pretty strong posse just to round him up!

III

Some Deer Facts

Every naturalist should possess an enquiring mind and have a keen pair
of eyes and alert ears. It is necessary to know something of the habits
of the bird or beast he watches and to build on to this knowledge with
personal observation. The great questions 'Why?' and 'Where?' become
very relevant. They can be answered only in terms of animal behaviour –
not human behaviour. But, of course, in Britain, human behaviour is the
greatest single factor which influences the lives and actions of so many
creatures. The little that wild animals may know of human beings rarely
reflects much credit.

There are four main species of deer in Great Britain – Red, Roe, Fallow
and Sika. In addition there are two minor species – Muntjac and Chinese
water deer. Of the four main species of deer, Roe are the smallest, standing slightly over two feet at the shoulder. Their winter coat is a mouse-
grey with a prominent white rump. Roe have no visible tail, although
adult females have a short white anal tuft. In summer the rump patch
becomes buff, and the coat of both sexes turns foxy red. Unlike the other
species, the bucks grow their antlers during the winter and they are in hard
horn during the summer months. The antlers normally have six tines or
points (three each side), nine inches being a good length for an adult antler.

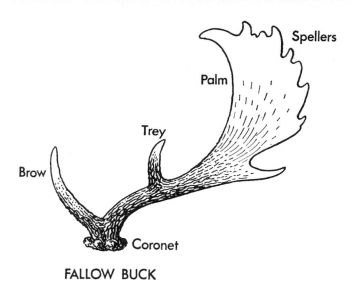

FALLOW BUCK

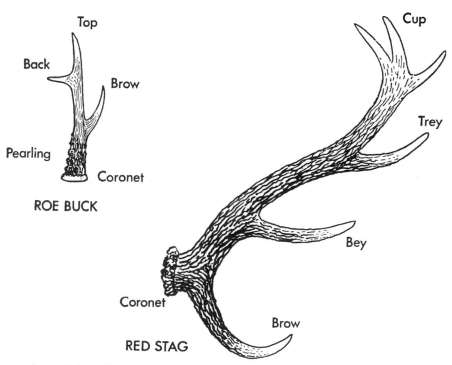

ROE BUCK

RED STAG

Antlers of the Fallow and Roe bucks and the Red stag. The bey and trey tines (or points) are also spelt bez or bay, trez or tray. The brow tine is also called the front antler and the trey tine in a Fallow buck an 'advancer'.

Male Fallow deer are readily distinguished from other British deer because their antlers are palmated. They carry brow and trey, but not bey tines (see diagram). They stand about three feet at the shoulder, the does being three or four inches less. In the summer the coat is very heavily spotted. The normal winter coat is mulberry coloured, but black or white Fallow deer are common, and the menil or spotted type occurs frequently, especially among park deer.

One of the main distinguishing features of Fallow deer is the tail, which is nine inches long – the longest of all these species. It is white underneath and black on top.

Sika are about the same height as Fallow, but are rather less 'leggy', being more thickset. The stags normally carry eight points (four each side), but ten-pointers do occur. The antlers are somewhat similar to those of Red stags. The summer coat is a dark brown with spots which are much less obvious than those of Fallow. The rump patch is white (like Roe in winter), but the six inch tail is distinctive. Sika stags appear to be quite black in winter, although the hair is actually a silver black. They carry a thick mane. In both sexes the ears are smaller than Fallow and both sexes have a distinctive grey V on the face.

Red deer are much larger than the other species. Stags are over three and a half feet at the shoulder, and the hinds over three feet. Their length from nose to tail is well over six feet for stags and five feet for hinds, compared with five feet for Fallow bucks and four and a half for Fallow does. A Red hind's face is long and pointed. The tail is shorter than both Fallow and Sika, and is a brown colour. The colour of the coat varies. In summer 'dun' or buff colour is common, or it may be a dark red–brown. In winter greyish brown or grey is most frequent.

The antlers should carry brow, bey and trey tines with three on top, making a 'royal'. But eight-pointers are common and where park blood has been introduced, or where food is exceptionally good, sixteen and even twenty points may occur.

The shape of a Muntjac is pig-like, with head carried low, the highest part being the middle of the back – twenty-two and a half inches. His tail, which is five inches long, is a pale fawn colour on the upper side. The antlers of Muntjac consist of two spikes set on long pedicles carried in line with the deer's forehead. When adult they bear two short points (one each side). The length is only four to five inches. The antlers may be cast at any time of the year. They live singly or in pairs, like Roe. There are two races which interbreed – the Indian race and the Reeve's, which is a brighter red in summer coat. The most interesting feature of the Muntjac is the pair of tusks which point downwards from the upper jaw. They are quite sharp, and they can inflict a nasty cut. Usually one 'cleave' will be markedly longer than the other and this makes the tiny 'slots' very distinctive. Muntjac do some damage by browsing small forest trees, but it is much less than that done by the larger species of deer.

The Chinese water deer has no antlers, but both sexes have tusks. The shape of these deer is distinctive, because they carry their rumps high like sheep compared with the pig-like backs of Muntjac. Chinese water deer are very rare in Britain, being confined to Bedfordshire, Berkshire and north Hampshire. The majority of both Muntjac and Chinese water deer have originated from Woburn, Bedfordshire, the Duke of Bedford's property.

Red and Roe deer are indigenous to these islands, although man has moved them around a great deal. Fallow were almost certainly introduced by the Phoenicians and subsequently on a wide scale by the Romans. Being very amenable to park conditions, and having venison of high quality, they are the principal species to be kept in deer parks. Many feral Fallow deer have originated from escapes from deer parks. Two World Wars, with the tremendous pressure for the maximum food production out of every available acre, brought about the closure of many parks and the reduction of others. Many park deer were eliminated, but it was not unusual for a small proportion to escape. Thus the feral stock of Fallow deer is very mixed. Yet many localities have types of Fallow deer with their own characteristics – broad or narrow palmation, heavily split or forked palmation, good or bad brow tines, heavy or poor body weight or a preponderance of one or other of the four main colour phases: true fallow, menil (spotted), black, and white. A long-haired type has turned up in Mortimer forest. A similar type has been recorded in the Loch Lomond area.

In some areas it used to be the practice to hunt carted deer – that is a deer set loose for the purpose. At the end of the day these hunted deer were usually recaptured without difficulty, for hounds do not harm them. But occasionally one was not retaken and went free to swell the numbers already wild. In Thetford Forest the magnificent herd of Red deer is believed to have originated in this way.

Japanese Sika deer were not introduced until the latter part of the last century. They have become established in the wild state at comparatively few places.

It is a curious fact that deer, the largest wild land animal in Britain today, have been the Cinderella among creatures studied by naturalists and, with the exception of Red deer in Scotland and one or two Roe areas, by sportsmen, too. Almost all over Europe deer are treated with the greatest respect – almost with reverence; they are shot only by humane and sporting methods after strict observance of a traditional etiquette, which may vary from country to country, but which is everywhere of very real importance. Yet in Britain, a country which takes a just pride in her attitude to the humane treatment of animals, where there have been strict game laws for generations, deer are often regarded as vermin and treated with scant regard for their sufferings.

The First World War was responsible for the increase of deer in England. The heavy wartime fellings brought about the birth of the Forestry Commission in 1919. By the 1930s State planting on a large scale was in full swing, and many private estates had made excellent progress in replanting their areas of felled woodlands. The plantations began to form ideal cover for the deer which had escaped from parks and also for those already established in the countryside.

The whole process was repeated with the Second World War, with the major difference that the earlier plantations were already in the thicket stage – and very few staff were left to observe what was happening. In short, conditions were perfect for a rapid build-up of deer numbers.

How is it that deer, which are relatively large animals, are so often unnoticed? In the New Forest, where deer have been a very important part of the fauna since before William the Conqueror, I have heard it said many times: 'I have lived in the New Forest for years and never seen a deer!' There are two reasons for this. First, deer movements take place mainly at dawn and dusk, whereas most humans take their exercise in the midday sun. The second reason is that human beings are noisy creatures. Very few can walk silently. Those who are not countrymen are remarkably unobservant, and it needs a trained eye to pick out

SIKA STAG
October

RED DEER
STAG Winter

FALLOW BUCK
September

ROE BUCK
Early November

The view of deer most frequently seen.

a deer standing still in the shade of holly bushes or the shadow of oak coppice. In any case, most of those that may have been in view fade away silently, like shadows, on the noisy approach of humans.

But deer leave their 'signs'. These are the 'slots', or imprints of their 'cleaves' and their 'fewmets' or droppings. From these it is possible to assess the sex and, to some extent, the age, and also the numbers. Early in the morning in the dew, or during the day on grass and herbage, deer leave their 'foil' – that is, the sign of their passing. The trail through dew is obvious; the slight depression of grass and herbage is not so obvious, especially during dry periods – but it is there for the trained eye to see.

Other signs to be looked for are signs of browsing. Grass will be cropped. The tops of young trees may be eaten. Here it is necessary to note that a deer, because it has front teeth only on the lower jaw, tears rather than clips its food. A hare will cut off the tops of young trees as neatly as if they had been cut by secateurs. The same tree eaten by a deer will show frayed edges to the cut. A hare will often leave the top lying on the ground, but a deer does at least eat it.

There is a classic example of the mistakes which can arise in assessing deer damage. A young plantation of Japanese larch was found to have been seriously damaged. The foreman called in the forester. The forester was furious to see his larch ruined so he called in the Pests Officer. There was a deer park not far away and feelings ran so high that consideration was given to the possibility of making a claim on the owner of the deer park. Eventually the Forestry Commission game warden was called in to give advice as to where to place high seats for shooting the deer.

He very quickly pointed out that there were absolutely no signs of deer in the area: there was not a single slot and no fewmets. But everywhere there were runs and paths and droppings of mice. He was able to demonstrate that all the damage had been done by long-tailed field mice!

So, in looking for signs of deer, it is necessary to be very careful and very observant. In the spring the ends of bramble shoots will give a very good indication of the deer stock, for all deer love bramble shoots. In winter those trees which have any ivy growing up them should be examined. Deer will eat every leaf they can reach, even standing on their hind legs to reach higher. Fallow deer will strip ivy leaves up to a height of six and a half feet, but Roe do not reach nearly so high.

Another sign of the intensity of deer is found in the lower canopy of the tree crop. If deer have frequented an area for many years in fair numbers, there will be a grazing line in the foliage. This occurs at about three and a half feet from the ground in the case of Sika and Fallow deer, and is called the browse line. It is rather higher in the case of Red deer and about two and a quarter feet where only Roe deer are present.

In many areas of Britain one gets a similar line when rhododendron bushes are in flower. All the flowers will be stripped up to a height of about six feet, or even a little more. In this case the human animal and his family are responsible, damage being heavy at weekends and intense at Whitsuntide! But human damage is not confined to the rhododendron which is, anyway, the most troublesome forest weed. Any flowering shrub or plant is in danger of being broken and torn, or dug up. The spoor left behind – paper, tins, bottles, and worse – is one of the major problems of the countryside today.

The increase and spread of deer in England will continue for some considerable time. So long as the greater part of the forest area is in the young stage, the dense cover is especially favourable to deer. Where deer colonise new areas they may not be noticed for a year or so, and by then the numbers will have started to build up. There is such a serious lack of skilled and knowledgeable deer men in this country that there is an inevitable time lag between the discovery of a new deer population in an area and the organisation of efficient control.

In the case of Roe deer it is the young bucks which tend to spread outwards first. This is because the old bucks hold their territories – larger territories as they grow older – against newcomers. So the young buck wanders through the area seeking a territory of his own. If the forest is already fully stocked, then he will move out to seek new ground. If the new ground is unoccupied by deer, then of course he and any doe which may join him have the benefit of an untapped food supply and unlimited range. That is why it happens that the 'pioneer' Roe, or early comers who colonise a new area, often carry good heads.

Fallow deer are even greater wanderers than Roe. During the course of the winter, when food is scarce, they may spread out to new ground. Old does and old bucks tend to return to their favourite haunts, the doe coming back to the neighbourhood where she was born. Near there she will drop her fawn. The old bucks have their favourite haunts deep in the more dense parts of the forest, where they become very secretive while they are growing the new set of antlers. An old Fallow buck is by nature shy and furtive in any case, and he is an expert at keeping out of sight.

In the case of Fallow deer colonisation of new ground is usually achieved by the younger members of the herd. Among Red deer the stags are tremendous wanderers anyway. They may range twenty miles or more. In the rut they travel huge distances in search of hinds. That is one of nature's ways of preventing inbreeding.

I suspect that the pattern is similar with Sika deer, but I do not know. They are unpredictable deer, and they occupy favourite stretches of woodland, sometimes ignoring blocks of forest which appear equally well suited to their needs.

Prior to the 1962–63 winter, Muntjac were spreading fast from their main centres in Bedfordshire. Some of the places where they have turned up are so far removed from their normal haunts that one suspects human influence. Severe winters have a greater effect on these small, rather tender deer than on the other species.

All male deer, except the Chinese water deer, carry antlers – not horns. The antlers are cast and renewed annually, whereas horns are a permanent fixture on cows, antelopes, rhinoceros and goats. It is surprising that so many people get this simple fact confused, as well as the correct terms for describing the different species of deer. How often one hears (and even sees in writing) a Fallow buck described as a 'lovely stag with magnificent horns!' The correct terms are as follows:

Red and Sika deer: the male is a stag and the female a hind. The young are calves. Young males are brockets and staggies.

Fallow and Roe deer are referred to as bucks and does. As a rule Fallow does have single fawns, but Roe have twin kids. It is very rare for Fallow does to have twins. The stages in the development of male Fallow deer are first a buck fawn, then a pricket (at twelve months), followed by sorel, sore, bare buck, buck and great buck.

Basically antler growth depends on two factors – heredity and food supply. Both are very important. A male deer will pass on to its male offspring some of the main features of its own antler formation. Antler variation is very diverse, but the main characteristics are length and span, length of brow tines and, in the case of stags, length of bey (or trey) tines, shape (in the case of Fallow, breadth and shape of the palm particularly), colour and, in later life, thickness and weight.

Deformities in antler shape may result from a physical injury to the antler during the period of growth. More usually it is the result of an injury to a leg or testicle. In such cases the deformed antler will be on the opposite side to the part injured – thus a left hind leg shattered by shot will result in a deformed right antler. Internal parasites – lung worm, liver fluke, etc. – may also cause antler deformities.

Occasionally a male deer may not produce antlers at all at any stage of its life. Such animals are called hummels. As they are free from the strain of growing antlers, the body weight of a hummel is always above normal. Because of that a hummel will frequently beat off a normal stag when fighting.

Food supply affects the growth of antlers because, if the quality of feed is poor, the animal's body resources are inadequate to produce good strong antlers. Provided that the hereditary strain is satisfactory, the best antlers will be found where the food is best. The best type of feed will include a wide variety of trees, herbs and grasses, bramble leaves being an important food. As the quality of the vegetation is governed by the fertility of the soil, it follows that, other things being equal, the best antlers will tend to occur on good soils. Calcareous soils are especially favourable to antler growth because antlers are comprised mainly of calcium. It is obvious, too, that the greatest body weights come from areas where the food supply is good. Thus heavy antler growth and good body weight tend to coincide.

Deer eat their own cast antlers. They have no frontal teeth in the upper jaw; the incisors or outside teeth of the lower jaw are used to gouge out tiny slithers of calcium from the cast antlers.

The whole process of antler growth is a remarkable one. The date of casting varies with the locality; southern areas and those with good feed are usually in advance of northern areas or poor feeding areas.

In the New Forest Fallow bucks start casting on about April 25th. They are quite clean by August 25th (often earlier). So the whole process takes four months, the main growth period covering only three months. Old male deer cast their antlers before young ones, prickets usually being the last to do so. Therefore the old ones are usually clean first. But some prickets and sorels may clean early because their growth is smaller and finished sooner.

Red and Sika stags cast about a month before Fallow bucks. But the habit of the Roe buck in this matter is the most extraordinary. Roe bucks cast their antlers towards the end of October and into November. Therefore they have to grow the new antlers during the winter months when food is scarce. Moreover, in very severe winter weather it is possible for a Roe's growing antlers to be frosted following an injury, although this is rare. Roe become clean again from the end of March to mid-May.

I have never discovered any explanation for this habit, nor can I think of any satisfactory reason. Roe are indigenous throughout Europe and part of Asia Minor. If that were not so one might assume that they were more fitted to the southern hemisphere!

Antler development year by year will continue to improve until about the fifth or sixth year with Roe, the eighth or ninth year with Fallow, Sika and Red.

The age at which they mature varies very much with different localities and particularly with the food; where feed is poor they 'go back' earlier. Thereafter as the male deer gets older the antlers go back in length and sometimes in the number of points, though the thickness of the beam and coronet may not deteriorate. With Roe, more pearling may develop. As male deer age the pedicle becomes shorter, and the coronet is set closer to the skull with a marked forward slant. Until a deer is aged the number of teeth are the most certain way of telling its age. But after it is fully adult the only way to assess the age is by the wear of the teeth, the molars particularly. Even so this varies in different localities and is not entirely reliable.

Knowledge of deer is greater on the Continent than in England. But because of different conditions and the fact that the new habitats of deer in England are increasing and deer are spreading, Continental knowledge is not always applicable to English deer. Therefore in this country today there is a very wide field for study. To the sportsman-naturalist there are few more rewarding activities than the study of deer. And the very fact that such a study takes one into quiet places means that something of interest, be it animal, bird, insect or plant, is seen on almost every outing.

IV

Roses and Runner Beans

Roses and runner beans are favourite food plants, and considerable damage is done by deer each spring to gardens which are not deer-proof. One lady had deer droppings actually on her front doormat!

When deer take to marauding gardens, it is possible to scare them away by various means such as tin cans suspended on wire, coloured rags on string, creosote or other strong smelling repellents. Such means are temporary deterrents only. The deer will get used to them in a very short time.

One enterprising gentleman set up an alarm consisting of a piece of thin wire, a mousetrap, a battery and an alarm clock. When the mouse-trap went off the bell rang under his bed and he went charging out in his pyjamas with a loaded gun, ready to deal death among the deer. In another garden a large black cow was actually shot – but that's another story.

It is possible to shoot some, but such action is repulsive to any humane person because deer break into gardens at the time of year when there is a close season. Also it is not a cure, for others will take the place of the one which has been shot sooner or later. To shoot a buck when he is growing his antlers, or to shoot a doe heavy in young, may not necessarily involve cruelty; but it still goes against the grain with all true sportsmen. To shoot a doe from mid-May onwards, when the Roe drop their kids, involves the most gross cruelty. Females of all species leave their young for long periods, and a single doe is unlikely to be a barren doe (the few barren does which there may be usually consort with other deer of their own species). Anyone who has seen a fawn dying slowly of starvation, because its mother has been shot, would give a good many rose trees and runner beans to erase the memory of that pitiful sight.

It is impracticable for the owner of a forest to kill all the deer, and so long as there are deer present some will be certain to visit the gardens in the area during the spring. From a deer's viewpoint the temptation is irresistible, and once the habit has been formed it is very difficult to break, and it tends to get worse over the years, as deer are quick to learn from each other.

There is only one certain cure for marauding deer in gardens: that is to make the fence deer proof. Deer like to push through low places, therefore the lower part should be of rabbit, sheep or pig netting. Above that, strands of wire every six inches must be arranged so as to bring the height up to six feet. Cheap ex-W.D. wire can be used for this purpose. The total cost may be high, but it is no higher than the cumulative value of rare shrubs lost over the years. If it brings peace of mind and freedom from frustration it may be reckoned as a cheap investment.

In one garden, deer had been doing a lot of damage to rose trees. The young son of the house was an observant lad and keen on anything to do with nature. He picked up the slots of a Roe doe and followed her trail across the flower beds and through a gap in the hedge. The soil in the wood beyond the hedge was moist and soft so it was not too difficult for him to follow the tracks across the bare ride. From there they went along a narrow little path, fringed on each side by bluebells, now fading and beginning to set their green pods, their onetime glossy leaves yellowing. For their glory was now over; their annual task of flowering and setting little black seeds and making hundreds of thousands of tiny new bulbs was drawing to its natural conclusion.

After a hundred yards or so, the trail led to a shallow ditch. The animal had followed the line of the ditch, walking along the bottom for eighty yards and leaving clear slots in the damp soil. Then they ended. But young Robert picked them up again on a bank of bare soil. Here he was astonished to find other imprints of tiny cloven feet, so small that they might have been made with a nut picker. Beyond, the woodland opened out into a boggy area, now relatively dry; it was much overgrown with molinia grass and bog myrtle. There he found it quite impossible to pick out the tracks. However, he noticed one or two small sallow bushes which had been stripped of bark and were ivory coloured where the stem below had been laid bare.

For some time he wandered about searching carefully for signs of his quarry. Presently he paused by a small sallow bush. At the side of it was a patch of bare soil, dappled with the shafts of sunlight shining through the leaves. Suddenly he realised that the sun had gone behind a cloud, yet the dappled shadows remained. He looked closer and then, found himself looking into two large, brown eyes. He stood stock still, gazing in wonderment. 'A fawn!' he said to himself. 'What a beautiful creature!'

It was in fact a Roe kid and because it had only been born a few hours, it had no experience of mankind and therefore no fear. Robert made the mistake, which so many people make when they find a Roe kid, Fallow fawn or Red calf. 'It's been deserted and got lost. I must take it home.' He stooped down to pick up the small creature. As his hand touched it, it rose shakily on its spindly legs and stood trembling. The touch of his hand had awakened its instinctive fear.

When Robert grasped hold of it, it let out a piteous scream. Robert jumped backwards. He was horrified, and not a little scared. The kid stopped screaming as soon as he released it and started to stagger away on its spidery legs. Behind him Robert heard a slight sound and then a bark, 'Boh!' He wheeled around, not knowing what to expect. Standing in the open about forty yards from him was a Roe doe. As he looked at her she stamped her foot and then ran a few yards and stood behind a bush. She was torn between her natural fear of man and her instinct to protect her kid.

Robert, who had never seen a deer before, was uncertain. He did not want to touch the kid again, partly because he had been upset when it screamed, and partly because he was half afraid of the doe. To him her timid movements appeared to be a little menacing. So he turned and went home to fetch his mother, and he brought her back to see

the kid. But there was nothing there. The doe had taken her young one right away. All he could point out was a small, round bed where the kid had been lying, and its tiny footprints.

The food of deer is most variable. They are grazing animals, therefore grasses, herbs, shrubs and fruits form their main diet. But they also eat lichens, mosses and fungi. Some grasses are eaten less than others, molinia and the holcus grasses ('Yorkshire fog') are not taken avidly; it is the seeds of sedges which are eaten. When food is scarce rushes will be eaten, too. Wild roses and brambles are favourite and important food plants. Heather, bilberry and gorse shoots are eaten, while ivy, holly and green yew are sought in hard weather.

Plants which do not seem to be eaten are: evening primrose, wild sage, foxglove and ragwort, and the leaves of daffodils. Bracken is sometimes nibbled, and the male fern is eaten with relish.

Most broad-leaved trees are much sought after, especially at the time of flushing in spring. Sweet chestnut, red oak, elm, oak, beech and poplar are all favourites, but birch is eaten only if food is scarce. Most conifers are eaten or 'browsed' all too greedily, and none is immune. Roe deer eat larch rather more readily than the other deer species. Deer have an unfortunate habit of seeking out and eating any new species, which is in short supply, perhaps because they like change. Certainly where there is a wide variety of food available the quality of the stock of deer is best.

Blackberries, bilberries, mountain ash and other berries, crab apples, sweet chestnuts, acorns, and beech mast are all sought in due season. Of these, the last four are special favourites. To a large extent the crop of acorns determines the natural resistance of deer to hard weather in the winter, though that applies more to Fallow deer, which are primarily woodland creatures, rather than to Red. The main habitats of Red deer in Britain do not often include a big acreage of hardwoods.

The bark of many different species of trees is eaten. This is called 'stripping'. Many hardwoods, especially when thin barked, are thus damaged, and the bark of yew, holly, thuja, Lawson cypress, Norway spruce, tsuga and sometimes pine is also eaten. Red deer do serious damage to Lodgepole pine by stripping the bark.

On farm land deer graze the pastures and may do a considerable amount of damage to fields from which stock is excluded in order to promote 'the early bite'. They also damage hay, young wheat and corn, although early damage to young cereal crops usually does not prevent a good crop developing. When corn is ripening deer may do much damage. This is partly because they will lie up in such crops, and partly because they are feeding on the vegetation in the bottom and trample the corn at the same time. They also eat the ears of grain. Root crops of sweeds, turnips, mangolds, sugar beet and potatoes are also eaten.

It is obvious, therefore, that by grazing, browsing or stripping deer may do very considerable damage. In forests male deer of all species will do much damage with their antlers by 'fraying' young trees. All four main species of deer cause such damage, first when rubbing off their velvet, then when marking out their territories, and lastly in play.

There are various commonsense measures which a forester can take in order to reduce damage or to make control of the stock of deer easier. In the original planting some thought should be given to the future deer problem in the area.

In Red deer country if one sits high up on the hill and studies the glen below, the main deer paths can be seen almost as clearly as footpaths marked on a map. These paths lead to and from their main feeding grounds and also to the main passes in the hills and the main crossings of the burns. All too often afforestation schemes are planted with a sort of grid system of rides and compartment boundaries, which completely ignores these deer paths. This is a bad mistake. The deer will not be diverted from their age-old routes by the planting of trees, and damage will be severe alongside these deer paths. But when the surrounding trees grow up into the thicket stage, the deer will pass through the area in complete concealment, and the task of the stalker will be much more difficult. If the main paths are left as rides and tracks, then damage will be less, and the stalker will have reasonable visibility to shoot, even when the forest is in the most dense stage. Furthermore, these deer paths often follow an easy gradient and a direct route which is equally helpful to man.

Extra space for shooting should be left at the main passes and river crossings, and there is a case for leaving some of the main feeding areas unplanted. All these measures aid control in later years. And efficient control means greater revenue from the sale of venison and from shooting trophy and cull heads. It is also unwise to plant up the main rutting stands for the simple reason that uneconomically severe damage is inevitable on rutting stands.

Where fraying by male deer of any species is a serious trouble, then the wise forester will leave odd stems of weed species such as sallow, birch and mountain ash, especially on ride sides, or beside open glades. Many of these will be frayed instead of the planted tree crop.

When a block of the forest reaches the brashing stage – that is when the lower branches are due to be removed – it is a mistake to brash the whole block at one time. This will cause the deer to change their local habits and make more difficulties for the stalkers. If the brashing of the odd acre or two is deferred as long as possible, then the deer will continue to lie up in these thickets during the day time and the stalker will know exactly where to find them.

When weeding young crops foresters often like to see their young trees kept entirely clean and bare of all vegetation. In many cases this is a wasteful practice and in deer country it will increase the damage by browsing. It is important to leave as much cover as possible, provided the planted crop can get through. Brambles and birch afford very good protection from deer and usually only a light weeding is needed anyway.

There are not so many aids to the reduction of damage on farm lands. As already stated, a complete deer fence is the right solution for gardens, and also perhaps for especially valuable farm and forest crops (e.g. research plots). But the expense of complete fencing is prohibitive for large acreages. It is important to keep the bottom of hedges, or fences, thick. In the case of fences, or gaps in hedges, sheep netting is the best.

Lastly there is the electric fence. The ordinary type of electric fence, with one thin wire, is unsatisfactory. Sooner or later the deer will be stampeded through the wire. The resulting tangle is beyond the ordinary man's patience to unravel. But there is a type of electric fence which is made up of thin fuse wire wound around a polythene core. If deer stampede through this the wire breaks. A loose length carried in the pocket can be tied in quite simply to repair the break.

But none of these measures is adequate without the proper control of the stock of deer as well.

A Roe buck does no damage with his antlers when in velvet. It is not until he starts to clean off the velvet that he does some damage. This cleaning process is rapid, and the amount of damage done at this stage is slight – two or three trees. The greatest amount of fraying damage is done from this period onwards, for a very different reason. As soon as a Roe buck's antlers are clean he starts to mark out his summer territory. This he does by making scrapes with his forefeet, by rubbing his scent glands against bushes and trees, and by fraying small trees with his antlers. The point is that the size of the territory depends on the age, strength and vigour of the buck. A mature buck in his prime, and an old buck, especially before he starts to 'go back' in condition, will hold the largest territories, and they will fray the smallest number of trees. A young buck will hold only a small territory, but he is always trying to make a position for himself in the world, and therefore will fray very many more trees in his territory.

Hence it is obvious that if damage is to be kept to a minimum, very careful selective shooting must be carried out. Good young bucks may be left in territories where the crop is not vulnerable to damage. But in vulnerable areas an old buck in his prime should be left in possession. He will save the area from serious damage more effectively than a rifle. Shoot him and his territory will be split up, maybe into three. In the process there will be a great deal of fighting and many disputes, all accompanied by fraying of the crop.

The right time to shoot Roe bucks is in the summer from May to September. Then each buck has his territory well defined. He goes round it methodically twice a day, and there he may be found, day after day. The stalker should be able to examine the territory and to decide whether the buck should be shot because he is doing harm, or left because he is holding a large territory. Then he must choose a suitable vantage point when the wind is right and from where he will be reasonably certain of obtaining a good view of the buck and of shooting him painlessly with a rifle, if that is necessary. Where sport and quality of the stock of deer are the only considerations, it may be desirable to shoot the old buck to make room for a promising young buck. And in practice a good stalker will make such decisions in the light of local circumstances.

But it cannot be emphasised too strongly that no one can do this in winter. The bucks are not on their territories. Even if they were they could not be shot selectively because their antlers are not developed; and perhaps the most cogent reason of all, they are almost entirely nocturnal!

STATUTORY OPEN SEASONS FOR DEER

Species	Sex	England and Wales	Scotland
Red	Stag	1 Aug. to 30 April	1 July to 20 Oct.
	Hind	1 Nov. to 28 (29) Feb.	21 Oct. to 15 Feb.
Sika	Stag	1 Aug. to 30 April	1 July to 20 Oct.
	Hind	1 Nov. to 28 (29) Feb.	21 Oct. to 15 Feb.
Hybrid (Red × Sika)	Stag	No legislation	1 July to 20 Oct.
	Hind		21 Oct. to 15 Feb.
Fallow	Buck	1 Aug. to 30 April	1 Aug. to 30 April
	Doe	1 Nov. to 28 (29) Feb.	21 Oct. to 15 Feb.
Roe	Buck	1 April to 31 Oct.	1 April to 20 Oct.
	Doe	1 Nov. to 28 (29) Feb.	21 Oct. to 31 March
Muntjac Chinese Water Deer	Both sexes	There is no legislation. However, as recommended by BDS the Open season should be 1 Nov. to 28 (29) Feb.	

Notes: 1 In England and Wales, only Roe bucks have a season different from other male deer. All females have the same season.
2 In Scotland all females, except Roe does, have the same season.

Details of all further legislation may be attained from the British Deer Society. The use of shotguns is strongly deprecated and is strictly limited. In Scotland the .222 rifle is legal, but not in England.

V

The Rut

The rutting habits of the different species of deer are of considerable interest. They are also most important, because it is at this time that the oldest males may be seen, because they become bold. Also male deer which have not been seen before in the area often turn up, either because they have come in from another estate or because they have been overlooked.

It is during the rut that the best opportunities occur to cull (or thin out) male deer selectively. It is most important to shoot bad specimens on the rutting stands before they pass on their weaknesses to future generations.

Roe deer are the first to rut. The rut occurs during the last week of July and the first week of August, but in some localities does may come in season earlier and in the New Forest sometimes Roe bucks may be seen running does by mid-July.

In the case of Roe the pattern of behaviour throughout the summer has to be understood, as this leads up to the rut. When the bucks first start to fray in April and May, this activity takes place on the winter ground. In hill country the summer areas may be well away from the winter ground, and even in such an area as the New Forest there is a good deal of change during May. Also at this time the family parties split up. The previous year's kids, both male and female, are driven out. By June bucks which were located in April on their winter grounds may well be in quite different areas.

From May onwards the bucks select their territories. Their summer racks, or paths, are much less evident than the winter racks. These territories are marked, as I have said, by fraying stocks and scrapes made with the fore foot at the base of the fraying stock. More often than not the boundary of the territory will follow a natural feature such as a ride or stream. Sometimes there is a buffer zone between adjoining territories – a sort of 'no-man's-land' not claimed by either buck. Each buck will visit his main fraying stocks at least once every day, leaving the scent from his special scent glands on the various fraying stocks and also on trees which are not frayed.

Any visiting buck will pay most particular attention to the fraying stocks of the resident buck. There is little doubt that from his close examination he forms a very good idea of what sort of a buck is the resident. It behoves a stalker to pay equal attention to these fraying stocks for he, too, can form an opinion as to the type of buck and his movements. Also it is only after he has worked out the territory that he can make a certain plan for outwitting the buck.

The does drop their kids from the middle of May. By July the doe, still of course accompanied by her new kids, has joined a buck and she will then live within his territory. Buck and doe will seldom be out of earshot of each other, although the casual observer may not see more than one or the other.

As the doe comes in season she will utter a plaintive piping 'peep' and this attracts the immediate attention of the buck. A considerable chase ensues, the buck grunting as he pursues the doe. Often the doe will run in a very small circle, centred on a stump or bush, or sometimes in a figure of eight. These Roe 'rings' will be used at intervals so long as the doe remains in season. It is the doe that chooses the site of these rings. Mating takes place from time to time when the doe stops running and a buck may cover the doe many times. If the doe survives until the following rut she will use precisely the same rings the next season. Hence it is important to note the position of these rings. Not all Roe use rings and in some forests rings are rare.

When the doe utters the plaintive mating call, other bucks will be attracted to the area. But because they know that the buck of the territory will be with the doe, their approach is extremely cautious. In fact a buck hearing a 'peeping' doe other than his own will stalk her upwind very carefully.

A young doe which has not bred previously will be frightened by the pursuing buck and in this case she will utter quite a different high-pitched call: 'Pee-you'. This call has an immediate effect on other bucks within earshot. They throw discretion to the winds and come very fast to the area.

These two calls may be used by stalkers to bring bucks out into the open. It is very exciting and often produces an old buck with a magnificent head which was unknown previously. It is a good method for culling rubbish, but good bucks should not be shot by this means.

Recently two experts were demonstrating the various calls to each other. To his great annoyance one of them was able to produce only a squeak like a mouse. He was quite put out. I met him the next day. He said: 'I've found out what was wrong with my Roe call. There was an earwig inside it! When I tried this morning it nipped the tip of my tongue!'

Bucks may be called outside the rutting season by imitating their alarm note, which is a short bark: 'Boh'. As a matter of fact, when really alarmed a Roe does not usually bark – he just disappears. So when he barks it represents a question mark in his mind. If the stalker answers, then the buck's curiosity cannot be contained. Almost certainly he will turn and reply. Usually he gives a good chance to be seen and, if necessary, shot. A doe, or a young buck, give a higher pitched bark than that of an old buck. It is important to answer a young buck with a young buck's note and an old one with a deep note. A young buck will not come forward readily if he thinks that an old one is present and an old one may choose to ignore a young one. But each will react at once if he thinks that another buck of similar strength is in his territory. Barking will not necessarily alarm other Roe within hearing. But it may start them barking, too. Barking by Roe is most frequent during the period April to August.

When the rut is over the bucks are exhausted. They lie up in dense cover and do not show up until mid-September.

It is a very curious biological fact that, after mating, development of

the Roe embryo is delayed until January. (A similar delayed implantation occurs in seals and badgers.) Thus, initial development is brought nearer to that of other deer which rut in October. At this time of year there is also a 'false rut'. Roe bucks once again are much in evidence, chasing the does. It may well be that a doe which has not been mated at the normal time will mate during this period of false rut and then embryo development is normal.

The rut of the Red deer is a very different matter and the general pattern of behaviour is better known than is the case with the other species. The master stag possesses himself of as many hinds as he can gather and his main concern is to hold his harem together and at the same time ward off any other stag that may challenge him. As each hind comes in season, so he will run her and cover her.

From time to time the stag will throw back his antlers so that his open mouth is pointing slightly upwards and emit the roar which is such a feature of Scottish deer forests during the rut. It is an impressive wild sound which carries a considerable distance.

The same rutting areas tend to be used year after year and the master stag will use the same wallows each year. When wallowing he throws the peaty soil over his back with his antlers, while lying semi-submerged. When he reappears he is almost black.

On the fringe of the rutting area young stags will be found hoping for a chance to cut out a few hinds when the master stag's attention is distracted. These lesser stags take very good care to keep out of the way of the master.

At this time of year stags cover great distances in their search for hinds which may be held by a beast smaller than themselves. When the master stag is challenged by a newcomer of similar proportions a pro-longed fight may ensue. The master stag, who is on his own home ground, uses the unevenness of the ground to his own ends when the fight starts. If he has the advantage of slope and weight then the fight may be over quite quickly in his favour.

A stag which has held his hinds from the start will begin to grow weary towards the end of the rut, when he may be replaced by a younger or smaller stag that would not have stood a chance earlier.

It is curious that the rut of wild Fallow deer does not seem to have been given much attention by naturalists and sportsmen. It is often assumed that the pattern is the same as the Red deer rut, but that is not so, although, of course, there are some similar features.

Towards the end of September the neck of the Fallow buck becomes very swollen and thickened and the adam's apple becomes very pro-nounced. This thickening of the neck also occurs very markedly in Red and Sika stags and rather less markedly in Roe bucks. During September Fallow bucks become restless and roam far afield, for it is not often that a buck ruts on his home ground. Therefore strange bucks turn up in areas where they have not been seen before. Indeed some are seen only during the rut. In the New Forest only one black Fallow buck was known*, and he had never been seen outside the rutting period. It was believed that he came in from an estate well to the north of the forest.

The rut takes place on traditional rutting stands, many of which have been used since time immemorial. But there are also lesser rutting

---

* *In 1968.*

stands, which do not have the same status as the traditional stands. If the master buck is shot on a traditional stand he will be replaced. But if the buck in possession of a lesser stand is shot the stand may not be used again. As a rule the same buck will use the same stand year after year. In areas where there is considerable disturbance he will have alternative smaller rutting stands, to which he will move if disturbed. There may be four or five of these and the last ones may be regarded as 'emergency' stands, which are used only when all else fails.

Before the rutting stands are occupied the Fallow buck will mark out his territory, which will include the rutting stand of his choice. He does this in much the same manner as the Roe bucks do, by means of fraying stocks. His scent glands are also active at this time so that his scent is left on the fraying stocks. The first 'groaning', as the mating call of the Fallow buck is known, is usually heard early in October. This rutting call is a throaty grunting, almost belching sound, given continuously for varying periods. The tone varies with the age of the buck, young bucks' voices being higher pitched than the much deeper notes of old bucks. The sound is made with the head pointing slightly downwards (in contrast to the Red stag posture), but the head is jerked upwards as the sound is emitted through the open mouth. The sound does not carry nearly as far as the roar of the Red stag. On a still day Fallow bucks may be heard a little over half a mile.

Once groaning has started the buck's territory is drawn in towards the central rutting stand and he will make a number of scrapes, on to which he urinates. The soil from these scrapes is plastered on to his flanks by means of his antlers. By this time the buck is possessed of a very pungent odour, obvious even to the human nose!

Now the main difference between the rut of the Fallow and that of the Red is that in the case of Fallow deer the does draw in to the buck, and the buck makes no serious attempt to round them up, or to hold them, as does a Red stag with his hinds. Therefore the Fallow buck has to advertise his presence on the rutting stand by means of groaning and by his pungent odour, so as to attract the does to him. At the same time his activities act as a warning to other bucks. It is the rutting stand which the master buck possesses and defends.

By mid-October, the area of the rutting stand is in the region of some sixty yards long by forty wide. At the height of the rut it may become even smaller. Within this area the buck parades up and down, groaning almost continuously for many hours on end. Among the does which draw into the area there is an atmosphere of intense excitement. They run hither and thither and sometimes make a whickering sound, while in the background lesser bucks move restlessly backwards and forwards, although they dare not come too close.

When the deer on a rutting stand are disturbed they disperse. When all is quiet the buck will begin to groan again on an alternative stand; some of his does will return to him. Others will join the next nearest buck which can be heard groaning.

If another great buck comes upon the scene, sometimes because he has been disturbed from his own rutting stand, he will walk slowly into the arena. The master buck may instigate a fight at once. More often he walks behind the newcomer, almost indifferently, though no doubt he is sizing him up. Slowly he will edge up until his shoulder brushes the hindquarters of the new buck. The reaction is usually instantaneous; the new buck wheels round and the antlers of the two interlock with a loud crash. Such a fight is an inspiring sight as the two bucks bring into full play their great neck muscles, while the muscles of their hindquarters quiver as they strain and struggle. But they rarely do serious physical damage to each other, although the mental dejection of the vanquished buck is obvious from his whole demeanour.

Such a fight is for possession of the rutting stand and not the does. But as the does come into season, so they are served, sometimes after a long chase which may take both deer well away from the rutting stand. It is very rare to witness a buck covering a doe. In my own experience, although there is intense activity on the rutting stands from dawn onwards, I have not seen a doe served earlier than 9 a.m. and the few other people whom I know to have witnessed this have seen it at various times between noon and 3 p.m.

It is generally assumed that all species of deer normally mate at night. In 1965 I saw Roe, Red and Fallow in the act of mating: Roe on July 27th in the evening, Red on October 9th at 6 p.m., and Fallow on October 21st at dusk and on October 22nd at 9 a.m.

Fresh does draw in to the stands to take the place of those which have been served, and towards the end of October the master bucks can no longer hold their own against lesser bucks. It follows that those does which are late coming into season are served by the weaker bucks. Therefore they will tend to bear late fawns of poor hereditary quality. There is a strong case for shooting such does on the rutting stands and this should certainly be done when the rut drags on into November, as it is then legal to shoot them.

There are several records of a buck killing a doe during the rut. This is said to happen if the doe has been served by another buck or if she will not stand. Does normally breed for the first time at twenty-eight months, but there are records of sixteen month old does mating and proving to be fertile. The gestation period is eight months.

A common factor with Roe, Red and Fallow is that the males eat practically nothing during the rut. Therefore they get very thin indeed and the venison deteriorates. The venison of a Fallow buck shot early in the rut, while still in good condition, is not tainted by the strong body odour, provided that skinning and dressing are done carefully.

Sika stags do not lose condition during the rut to the same extent as the other species. It may be presumed that they do not fast so continuously; and they drink more frequently than other deer. Sika deer are indeed much more unpredictable than other species of deer, but this is no doubt partly due to the fact that their habits in the wild state in Britain are not yet fully known.

My own observations of their rutting activities are far from complete and may not apply to areas other than the New Forest. However, the incomplete pattern which I have observed is as follows:

At the end of August stags are not very much in evidence; one is left with the feeling that a large portion of the male stock has disappeared. A month before the stags begin to call they go through all the motions of calling without any sound issuing from the mouth – or at best a faint 'ahh'. This may be because either the throat muscles or the vocal chords are not in a suitable condition.

In September the stags take up territories and begin to call. This rutting call is a fascinating sound quite unlike the call of any other animal which may be heard in British woodlands. If one is close enough to hear it, it starts with a sharp intake of breath, although this is not very often heard. Then follows a clear, almost bell like, whistle rising to a crescendo and then falling down scale. Often this ends in a guttural 'ahh'. The whole takes up some four seconds and is repeated three times (sometimes four) in fairly quick succession. There is then complete silence normally for a quarter of an hour, when it will be repeated – and one can set one's watch by the rigid timing. Individual stags have variable time intervals from ten minutes even up to half an hour; but a quarter of an hour is the usual.

At about the time that they start calling the stags make scrapes. These are very similar to a Roe buck's if one makes allowance for the difference in size between the two animals.

The most obvious activity, however, is the mark which they make on the trunks of trees. These marks are made by an upward thrust of the top points of one antler against quite a substantial tree. In the New Forest a conifer is always chosen. It is of not less than four inches in diameter, going up to ten inches or so. The damaged area may be nine inches long by five inches wide and it penetrates sometimes an inch or more below the bark. The tree is marked for life and the damage occurs on the first length of timber – the most valuable part. So it can be quite serious. No hardwoods are ever used for this purpose in the

New Forest, but on the Beaulieu Estate field maple is used freely.

I am not yet certain whether these marks signify the boundaries of one stag's territory (as with Roe) or whether they indicate his favourite stand; but I think they indicate his calling stand.

Apart from these stands Sika have traditional wallows. The same wallows are used year after year and they may be situated some distance from the calling stands, although they call freely at the wallows, too. Several different stags may use the same wallow, although the master stag will take immediate possession from lesser stags.

When a hind is in season as many as eight or ten stags will gather together, but the master stag will chase and take the hind.

The Sika rut is much more prolonged than the rut of the other species. They will be heard whistling from the end of September until the third week of November, and they have been seen to mate in January, though this must be most exceptional.

VI

Control — Theory

Where man has not upset the balance of nature the many species of ungulates are kept at a healthy level by their natural predators. In years when the quarry becomes scarce through some factor, such as disease, the predators also suffer in that they produce only small numbers of young. But in years when their prey is numerous, predators raise large families. By this rough-and-ready law of nature a remarkable balance is achieved.

In England there are virtually no natural predators of deer. Foxes will take Roe kids when they are small, but often the doe will be able to save one of her two kids from a fox. Roe normally drop two kids and when a doe is seen with only one, there is a strong presumption that the other has been taken. A Roe doe is capable of killing a fox, although this is a rare event. That great expert on Roe deer, Ken MacArthur, has witnessed this on two occasions. He has recorded the fact that at the time a Roe drops her kids, the insides of the cleaves of her fore feet develop razor-sharp edges for the defence of her young. By the autumn these have worn off. Few fawns or calves of other species are taken by foxes, but in Scotland a golden eagle may take some Red calves. Generally these are weaklings and a large proportion of the calves which reach an eyrie are found dead by the eagle.

Uncontrolled dogs also account for a few deer annually. However, for all practical purposes it can be said that there are no serious predators of deer in Britain – other than man.

It is also true to say that wild deer are not highly susceptible to widespread disease. They may suffer from lung worm, liver fluke and, in very wet seasons, from a form of foot rot. Tick-borne fever has also been recorded, but is believed to be extremely rare. Disease is not often a major factor affecting their numbers (except possibly in overcrowded deer parks).

It is thus obvious that unless numbers are properly controlled the stock of any area will increase until the food supply becomes inadequate for their support during the critical months of the year – January to March, which is the lean time for all wild creatures. When this happens some may move outwards, but many will die of starvation, accelerated by an increase in their internal parasites, which increase in nearly all species of animals when they become emaciated.

In the New Forest there is a record of no fewer than three hundred Fallow deer being found dead in one enclosure alone. That was in the year 1777 when there was an exceptionally severe winter.

In the winter of 1962–63 this might have been repeated. As it was, casualties occurred among the weak and the old, among late born fawns and fawns which had lost their dams too early. But as fairly heavy culling by proper deer control methods had been carried out, the main stock survived, although they lost weight. Fortunately there had been a good acorn and beech mast crop the previous autumn – a very important factor.

A large amount of holly and ivy was cut for the deer by the keepers and hay was also put out. However, wild Fallow deer do not take to hay readily and when they do, they only pick it over looking for clover and other broad-leaved herbs. Ivy is excellent food and holly is eaten readily enough, though they prefer it when it has wilted.

From the foregoing it can be readily understood that it is essential to cull deer annually in their own interest. Furthermore, it is essential to do so in man's interests – whether these be agricultural crops or plantations of forest trees.

Once after explaining these facts at a lecture I was asked: 'Why can't you catch and move the surplus deer to other areas?'

Let us suppose that this is a practical proposition. The surplus from area A is moved to area B, and the next year to area C and then to area D. By this time B has a surplus to add to that of area A and stock E and F. By the time X Y and Z are reached there is the surplus stock of the whole alphabet to be placed – which is, as Euclid said, absurd.

Let us get away from sentiment. Deer have got to be killed to be controlled. But let us also make absolutely certain that only humane and practical methods of control are used, and the issue must not be clouded by misrepresentation. To many countrymen it would sometimes seem that some people are more concerned to see that no man shall enjoy the ancient and traditional field sports of this country, rather than that humane methods should be practised.

Countrymen and sportsmen understand how to employ humane methods. So often it is the townsman who does the most atrocious things through ignorance. The worst cruelty, however, comes from those who seek to turn killing into profit, rather than sport.

It is unpleasant to write about the atrocious acts of agony which are perpetrated against the largest wild animal of our British forests. But unless the ghastly results of wrong methods become widely known, there is little hope for improvement, because much of the trouble is due to ignorance and thoughtlessness. For instance, because a man is an expert shot with a ·22 rifle, he may assume that he can kill deer with this rifle, and it is possible to do so. But he has no margin for the slightest error in placing the bullet. If the vital part is missed by only an inch, the deer will not be recovered. It will either die a lingering death or suffer pain for a considerable time before it gets better. It is, therefore, essential to use a rifle of sufficient power. The Deer Act (1963) bans all rifles less than ·240 or with a muzzle energy of less than 1700 foot pounds.

Shotgun wounds are among the most terrible, especially when shot sizes smaller than S.S.G. are used. (S.S.G. is the smallest size shot which is permitted under the 1963 Deer Act.) A deer has to be very close indeed to be killed cleanly with small shot; at longer ranges a man has to be a very poor shot to fail to put some pellets into a deer's body. It is a sad and terrible fact that a very high proportion of wild deer in Britain carry shotgun pellets, often of several different sizes, in their bodies.

These are very frequently found in the hind quarters.

Snares (which are illegal) are still sometimes used by poachers, and occasionally by farmers adjoining forest land. They cause dreadful suffering. Not infrequently a snared deer will break loose with the snare still around part of its body. It will die a lingering death. A fine Fallow buck, found in Parkhill Inclosure in the New Forest, had a snare around the brow tines and the lower jaw, so tight that the wire cut into the jaw-bone. Yet it could open its mouth enough to eat a very little food, thus prolonging its lingering starvation. At the same time, the bone of the jaw was callousing over the injury. Snares of an identical type were found on the west side of the forest and it is a fair assumption that this unfortunate buck had travelled nine miles in the process of dying.

Some of the injuries which are found in the New Forest are shocking. Last winter a buck was seen with part of its back bone protruding above its shoulders; one shoulder was broken and protruded like a man's elbow. After it had been killed it was found also that its skull had been fractured, but had healed. All these injuries were caused by shotgun wounds. Yet this deer had recovered so far as it was able and it ran several miles before being despatched by the buckhounds.

The proper and most humane method of killing deer is with a rifle.

There is probably no more exciting or rewarding form of sport to be had in Britain.

Total elimination of all deer in an area is impractical. For one thing, the cost is out of all proportion to the value of the result. And even if achieved, some deer will have been driven out of the area during the process and they will return in due course – or fresh deer will come from outside. Therefore, total elimination can be successful only if combined with the erection of a deer fence around the area. This is so costly as to be prohibitive under normal forest conditions. However, deer fences are essential for the protection of gardens and very valuable crops such as arboreta, or for research plots.

The object of control should be to prevent damage from getting out of hand, and to maintain a healthy stock of deer. In Britain landowners have been very backward in realising that a healthy stock of deer is an asset to an estate, and one which will bring in an appreciable financial return. For the demand for deer stalking is increasing and greatly exceeds the supply. The next twenty years will see very high prices being paid for the right to shoot trophy heads. In many parts of Europe the cash value of a good Red stag is £1,000, and the price obtained for shooting a cull is £100. The chief difficulty in Britain at the present time is the shortage of trained deer stalkers and the general lack of deer knowledge in the countryside. But progress is being made and it is only a matter of time before sufficient trained stalkers will be available to conduct sportsmen to their appointed quarry. This is being done already on many Forestry Commission forests and on some private estates, and there is no doubt at all that the financial returns will continue to rise.*

So it must be clearly understood that deer control is not a case of going into a forest and shooting deer. It is necessary first to know what stock of deer is on the ground and then to decide which deer should be shot. After that shooting may begin, great care being taken to shoot only those beasts which should be shot. An efficient stalker should know which individual deer he intends to shoot before he sets forth from his house.

Successful control depends on a sound knowledge of the biology and habits of the species of deer present, an intimate knowledge of their local habits, and an ability to make a quick assessment. A successful stalker must have the ability to observe all the signs very keenly and accurately

* See page 68.

and then to draw the right conclusions and finally to act correctly in the light of these observations.

The man with an itching trigger finger is quite unsuitable for deer control. Self-restraint is an essential quality. So is the ability to move quietly and *very slowly*; or to sit motionless for a long time.

Different species of deer require different tactics in order to outwit them. However, broadly, there are two main methods which apply to all species in any type of country. The stalker can either seek out his quarry – i.e. stalk it – or he may wait at a suitable vantage point for his quarry to come to him.

There are no short cuts to knowledge other than by spending every available moment on deer ground. The novice will gain most experience at first by sitting still and watching. In this way he will see more and learn more of the natural movements and behaviour of deer. He will find it useful to carry a notebook in which to write down the times and details of all deer seen. The ability to make a quick sketch of antler formation is also most useful.

He who hurries from point to point in the hope of seeing something around the corner will be disappointed. The odds are heavily weighted against him. A deer's main weapon of defence is its nose and then its ears and then its eyes. But any deer will spot a quick movement or an unusual sound (particularly a metallic sound). And, of course, any taint of human scent is the end of that foray. Deer can pinpoint a man's position from the smallest sound or the faintest scent.

When looking for deer it is the greatest mistake to assume that because no deer can be seen, no deer are present. One has only to sit on a deer seat overlooking an open area to find out that deer can appear suddenly right in the centre of the opening. How they have got there is often a source of great surprise.

The expert, when searching for deer in woodland conditions, does not expect to see one at once. His field glasses will first reveal a twitching ear, or the flick of a tail, or the tip of an antler. Or he may see only a small patch of hide which looks exactly like a shadow, or like a patch of bare soil. These are the things which catch the trained eye. A deer that has seen a man will often stand stock still, well knowing that it is more than half-hidden by a bush. In such circumstances a deer's patience is much greater than a man's. A novice, seeing nothing, will move first.

It is then that the deer will bound away and its panic-flight will alarm other deer in the area.

When the novice has begun to succeed in seeing and watching deer he should then aspire to a more intimate knowledge by trying to see the world through a deer's eyes – and ears, and nose. There is no better way to do this than to follow the deer paths. He will very quickly learn that these paths, although they appear to wander haphazardly, are actually very direct routes to and from the feeding and resting places. He will also notice that a deer standing on a deer path in cover can see other deer, or men, which are moving along an open ride, or the edge of a glade. It is always easier to see outwards from inside a plantation than inwards from outside. It is also the case that in cover a deer's eyes are much better placed for seeing than a man's. That is because most of the low vegetation will have been grazed by the deer to a line above its eye level. But a man's eyes are well above this level so that the intervening leaves obscure his view.

From the deer paths a knowledge of their slots and therefore of their mode of movement can be obtained. The slots also reveal size, sex, age and numbers.

Often a novice will say: 'I suppose I mustn't smoke in case the deer scent the tobacco.' If there is any danger of fire, then indeed he must not smoke. But otherwise there is no reason at all why he should not; in fact it is an advantage, because he will gain a better knowledge of wind eddies by watching the smoke. A deer that is in a position to smell tobacco will have gone long before the cigarette is lit – for the human scent is far more frightening than smoke. But in open country deer may see cigarette smoke and become alerted. Red deer are more sensitive in this respect than are the other species, old hinds always being suspicious. In hard weather I have known deer stand in the smoke of the woodman's fire within minutes of knocking-off time, while they nibbled the twigs and buds, or leaves, which had not been burnt. Deer very quickly get accustomed to normal forest operations and they also have a very accurate sense of time. They know at what time the forest workers leave and they turn up very soon afterwards. This happens when felling is taking place, because they like to browse the leaves, twigs or buds from the tops of felled trees.

Having gained a fair knowledge of the deer in the area and of their habits it is desirable to draw up a shooting plan. Ideally this should be based on a census. The best time to carry out a census is in March or April, when the cover is thin, and deer movements most active, because they tend to feed on open grass land at this time. A count by sexes and ages should be made and any unusual deer (for instance, white Fallow deer or male deer with deformed or odd-shaped antlers) should be noted. The census is likely to be an under-estimate by as much as 30 per cent. A census of male deer should be taken during the rut.

The next step is to prepare the actual shooting plan. Every person in charge of deer control must decide how many deer should be killed. Numbers are controlled by killing females; the quality of the herd by selectively killing males. It is generally accepted that an equal sex ratio is desirable – but a slight excess of females is acceptable, especially in areas vulnerable to damage by male deer.

If food is scarce, or damage is severe, or if there is a high proportion of tree crop in the vulnerable stage, it may be necessary to reduce the herd appreciably, and females will have to be shot hard.

As a rough guide the normal increase may be expected to be in the region of 33 per cent, therefore no reduction in the herd will be achieved unless a higher proportion than about 33 per cent of the actual stock is killed. If the stock is 100, then one can compile a diagrammatic table showing exactly the numbers by ages and sexes which should be killed. To maintain an even herd the kill will be seventeen male deer and seventeen female, thus:

		Males	*Females*
Over 10 years	2	(Trophy heads)	⎫
8–10	None		⎬ 4 old
7–8	1	⎫	⎭
6–7	1		
5–6	1		5
4–5	1	⎬ Culls	Ages indistinguishable
3–4	2		in the field
2–3	2	⎭	
1–2	4	⎫ Poor	4
Fawns	3	⎬ beasts	4
	17		17

These theoretical plans are all very well on paper, but if followed too precisely one may find oneself scheduled to shoot half a deer of an age class which is quite unrecognisable in the field! Therefore the plan must be elastic. Of course, it is unlikely that the sexes will be exactly equal to start with, therefore more of one sex than the other may have to be killed. Also the number of poor male deer on the ground next season may not coincide with those which it is planned to shoot on paper. However, it is most important to have some such plan to use as a working basis and then to put it into operation, using commonsense and knowledge of the deer on the ground. In practice as many as possible should be shot on, or near, the vulnerable areas (that is, those areas of plantation in a stage of growth most susceptible to damage).

Before one can begin practical control one must check one's equipment. For all woodland stalking field-glasses are essential, but for the open hill a telescope is better. The best glasses must have a wide field of view, good visibility for dull light and magnification of ×8. Many Roe stalkers wind insulation tape around the thick end to prevent that metallic click when they touch the rifle or thumb stick. A thumb stick is most useful to steady the rifle hand when taking a standing shot. A lanyard or cord attached to the thumbstick and to a buttonhole or belt, or to the strap of a bag, will enable the stick to be dropped if both hands are required for the use of glasses.

One's clothing should match the background of the country where one is stalking. In woodland a Loden coat, as worn in most parts of Germany and Austria, is perfect. Because it is made of mohair it does not make a scratching noise when one brushes against twigs. It is warm and waterproof.

An essential piece of equipment is a face mask and, when Roe shooting in summer, some form of insect repellent is desirable. A good sharp knife is necessary and a whistle is useful, but an empty rifle cartridge case can be used for this purpose, by blowing across the top.

★ *(See page 64.) Since this book was written, great advances have been made in the knowledge of deer management, and the efficiency of Stalkers carrying out control. Fees for stalking have increased substantially.*

VII

Control — Practice

Of the three main senses, sight, sound and scent, it is scent which is by far the most important when dealing with deer. By moving *very* slowly, literally only an inch at a time, it may be possible to approach deer when in full view. By moving very carefully and avoiding any unnatural sound, especially metallic noises, one may be able to approach quite near, although their hearing is very acute. But the smallest suspicion of human scent in the air will end the proceedings at once.

No one can ignore wind direction and all moves must be planned to take account of it. Due regard must also be paid to the effects of wind on the movements of deer.

Deer lying at rest prefer to choose a site from which they have a view down wind. They will lie with their backs to the wind. If there is a local eddy where they are lying, this will be obvious because they will be facing away from it. Deer feed into the wind and wherever possible they prefer to move upwind. When they have to move down wind they move fast: often at a gallop.

This elementary knowledge must always be in a stalker's mind.

The first thing to do in woodland areas and in flat country is to put up deer seats. These high seats may vary from an elaborate platform built into a large tree, with back and arm rests, to a simple, portable, folding seat. One must be reasonably comfortable and the seat must be firmly secured. If one is sitting on a knobbly surface with one's feet dangling in space one's limbs will go dead and it is impossible to keep still. Therefore a foot rest is essential, and an arm rest makes for steadier aim.

The objects of using a high seat are threefold: safety, because one is firing down at a safe angle; good visibility – one can see into ground cover very much better from a raised position; and no disturbance of deer, because deer do not look upwards and one's 'wind' is usually carried above them. The ideal height is from twelve feet to sixteen feet. If one is much higher than that one may be enveloped in dense foliage, unable to see anything. One must be able to see under the canopy. There is one seat in the New Forest put up by an enthusiastic keeper in the top of a very tall oak tree. It is no mean feat of physical endurance to reach it, and when the deer do show up they look like ants. So it is called the Eagle's Eyrie.

A seat should be sited so as to give an uninterrupted view over an open space. Deer spend a lot of time in cover at the edge of open glades, and it is therefore a great advantage to be able to see a little way into the cover at the other side of the glade.

The junction of four roads is not always a good place. Deer do not often follow a ride right through to a cross ride; they usually cut the corner some distance back and it is better to cover one well-used deer path than four unused rides. However, when a seat is sited to cover a particular deer path, the seat should be not less than forty or fifty yards away, so that the deer will pass broadside on. Often people make the mistake of putting the seat directly above a deer path. Even if the deer do not scent one's own trail to the seat, one is presented first with a head-on shot, then with the top of the deer's back and finally with his fast receding backside, all of which is very frustrating.

Different siting of seats will be required for the different species of deer, sometimes for the separate sexes, for different seasons and also for different times of day. Portable seats are very useful for Roe deer. If there is a shootable buck in a territory, a seat can be brought in and he can be taken; the chances are that it will not be necessary to take another buck there for some considerable period. But the regular paths and

passes of Fallow and Red deer will be used at the same periods year after year, and so permanent seats are justified for such places.

Very broadly, seats may be divided into those which cover feeding areas and those from which it is intended to intercept the deer as they pass to and from their feeding grounds. Seats may also be used for drives to rifles, using one beater who knows their runs. In any case one must decide in advance whether the seat is likely to be used in the evening or the morning, and it must be sited so that there is a reasonable line of approach. This needs much careful thought. It is not a bad thing to keep one's approach route swept clear of leaves, twigs, etc. Alternative seats, for use in different winds, are useful. When deer do not turn up, it is usually because they have winded one approaching the seat, or they have heard or seen one before one has reached the seat. The position of the sun must also be considered. It is irritating to be looking into the sun, especially when low on the horizon. The light should be behind the seat. The oldest bucks move in the poorest light and one needs everything possible in one's favour.

Sometimes the best used deer paths may pass wide of the only suitable clearing for shooting. These existing deer paths should be blocked with bushes and narrow paths cut to divert the deer to the glade. One can do a lot to draw deer to shooting points in this manner.

It is absolutely essential to pay particular attention to pruning branches and twigs which may obstruct the line of fire. A folding pruning saw and strong secateurs are most useful for this. The best way to test which branches need cutting is to sit on the seat and get someone to walk in a circle at about one hundred yards range and note every place where at first glance a shot seems possible. Then scrutinise every leaf that might divert a high velocity bullet. A man who has not done a lot of rifle shooting never seems to prune nearly enough.

There is one other most important point. All work connected with the erection of seats and pruning of foliage must be done in the middle of the day (if there is any intention to use it in the near future). How often this work gets left until the evening, because a man may have other important work to do during the day. By this disturbance at the time when the deer should be using the area, their local habits may be changed, and a good seat may be ruined for several weeks.

Finally there is the practical consideration of collecting one's deer after it has been shot. There is no point in placing a seat a mile from a hard track if there is an equally good site closer. Where access is bad, then it is a good idea for several rifles to combine by using several seats in one area at the same time. They can then help each other to pull out the dead deer. Also their combined observations should give a very good picture of the deer movements in that area.

All these considerations make it sound as though the erection of deer seats is highly complicated, but it is really a matter of using common sense. The final selection of the site is usually a compromise of fitting in as many desirable factors as possible. Until experience is gained it is better to start with portable seats which can be moved. Often a move of a few yards will make the difference between a poor seat and a good one.

In Red deer hill country it is exceptional to need seats. The majority of deer shot will be stalked. But it is also desirable to select vantage points overlooking deer paths and passes, rutting areas and wallows. The difficulty in Scotland is to kill enough hinds. During the hind shooting season a rifle stationed at a pass on the high ground can often kill several if he has a companion to move them off the slopes below. If it is known beforehand where it is intended to shoot them, then the pony man's work is easier when getting out the venison.

Having got to know the habits of the deer and having got one's deer seats ready and made one's shooting plan the moment for shooting the first deer draws near. But before this moment comes the stalker must have become thoroughly proficient in the use of a rifle of adequate (and legal) calibre. Above all he must be used to the trigger pull. Even so there is a world of difference between shooting accurately on the range and performing well in the field. Three considerations must always be present whatever the local circumstances:

First, Safety: there must be a safe background. The fact that deer are grazing unconcerned does not mean that there may not be a human or an animal within the danger zone. A high velocity rifle bullet will travel an immense distance.

Secondly, the Right Deer: one should know which beast it is intended to kill before one leaves home. If others turn up they must be carefully assessed and due restraint used if promising young or middle-aged deer are present.

73

Thirdly, a Clean Kill: long shots, difficult or trick shots must be resisted. If there is a doubt there is always tomorrow.

There are a few points which may help a beginner. Whether he is on a high seat, or on the ground, he must decide which directions are safe. It is then a good idea to estimate one hundred yards and to make a mental note of convenient landmarks at this distance. These may be a patch of bracken, a branch, a lump of earth or any object which it is easy to pick out quickly. Any deer beyond these marks must be left alone. But when the right deer does appear well within range, the stalker must be quite clear in his own mind exactly where he wants to place his bullet. It is important to have seen a deer gralloched and skinned so that the relative positions of heart, lungs, liver, stomach and bowels are known. It is useful to visualise the effect of the bullet not as a hole, but as a shaft, or arrow, which will pierce the deer. The point of exit is as important as the point of entry, because a deer is more likely to be standing in a somewhat oblique position and not exactly at right angles. The beginner should confine himself to the heart shot, though the neck shot is the most satisfactory because it is instantaneous. A head shot should always be avoided. A very slight inaccuracy may break the jaw, which is a horrible injury, often impossible to follow up successfully.

It is important that a comfortable shooting position should be taken up, whether sitting, lying or kneeling. The left elbow should be through the sling of the rifle to give extra steadiness, but on no account must the rifle barrel rest on any solid object. A certain miss will result if it does, because of flip. It is the left hand, supporting the rifle, which may rest on any convenient firm rest, or be given extra support by the use of a thumb stick.

At last, when the time comes to take aim, the safety catch is pushed forward quietly, the rifle is pressed firmly into the shoulder and the fore sight is raised steadily up the inside of the nearest foreleg until a point is reached somewhere between a third and a half of the width of the deer's body. The sight is held steady and the trigger squeezed. Sighting should be quicker than in the case of target shooting, but if the rifle cannot be held absolutely steady, then the shot must not be taken. Lower the rifle, rest, breathe evenly and then try again.

It is very important to memorise the exact spot where the deer is standing. It is essential to be able to find this precise place after the shot is taken. For, if there is a hit, pins (hair) and paint (blood) will be found there and these signs will give immediate information as to the placing of the bullet and its effect, heart blood being dark and lung blood being pale red.

At the shot the deer may drop dead on the spot where he stood, especially if hit just above the heart. But when a deer drops to the shot it is possible that he has been only stunned and one must approach with care. If he goes off with a headlong rush, indicating a heart shot, then he will drop dead between twenty and eighty yards or so. If the shot is behind the heart he is likely to move off slowly, giving time for a second shot.

It is annoying to miss, but the greatest misfortune is to wound a deer. Therefore one should only take what one regards as a certain chance. The need to account for a wounded deer must take precedence over all other considerations, and in this connection there is a real need to have a dog trained to follow and bay a wounded deer. Almost any breed can be trained for this work, but if the dog runs mute, then it is a good idea to attach a sheep bell to his collar.

VIII

Tales of Visitors' Deer

Sportsmen who are not used to shooting from high seats sometimes do not realise how exciting this can be, nor how difficult. Sometimes the deer is too close. At such times one scarcely dares to breathe, let alone move. Very slowly one may be able to bring the rifle to the shoulder; but if the deer, as so often happens, is in such a position that it is impossible to bring the rifle to bear without moving one's body, then that movement is fraught with great difficulty.

Then there is 'buck fever'. As the moment approaches when the buck (perhaps one which has been sought on many previous occasions) is about to present a killing shot, the excitement is so intense that it can be quite unnerving. Novices, even grown men, can start to shake all over when the great moment arrives. I have experienced this myself.

David, whom I was training in deer lore and the proper use of a rifle, at last had the opportunity to shoot a doe. I put him on a high seat near a place where half-a-dozen does came out to feed in a clearing each night. He did not have a shot, and when I joined him afterwards I asked him what had happened. 'Did no deer come out?' I asked.

'Yes, several.'

'Were they too far?'

'No, they were right under the seat.'

'What happened then, did you have a misfire?' I asked, for I was disappointed that he had not had his shot.

'Well,' he said, with a burst of frankness, 'it's all very well for you, you've shot hundreds of deer; the truth is my knees were knocking and my teeth were chattering, and I couldn't hold the rifle steady.'

David was extremely careful – as everyone armed with a high velocity rifle must be. He was so afraid of shooting the wrong deer, or firing a dangerous shot, or of wounding, that he would spend too long deliberating. Time after time a really good chance was lost through hesitation.

At last the day came when his luck changed. I had told him that he might take a poor pricket or a very bad buck.

At the shot I hastened down to where he was.

'Did you get one?' I asked.

'Yes, I think so. It rushed into a thicket.'

'What was it – a pricket?'

'Well, I'm afraid it's rather a good one.'

We found a very good buck. I was astonished and very cross.

'Whatever made you shoot that one?'

'Everyone's been pulling my leg and saying I'd never get one – so I determined I'd shoot the first I saw. But I didn't realise he was so good!'

Since then David has shot many a deer correctly in many parts of Britain. Success breeds success and he has become a good and reliable rifle shot. Most important, he is now an accurate assessor of quality.

★   ★   ★   ★   ★

For some years I have been co-operating with a Research Institute to provide material for investigating diseases in deer. The main line of investigation is to find out whether there is a link between diseases of deer and those of domestic animals: and whether immunity in deer might provide a lead for protection of domestic stock.

In order to carry out these investigations it was necessary to take blood samples, and other samples, immediately after the deer was killed. It was not always possible for the forest keepers to be spared from their routine jobs in order to obtain the required specimens. Therefore the director of the Research Institute, and a colleague of his, a charming lady who is a keen and experienced shot, assisted me in shooting the actual deer required. This had to be done at dawn and dusk.

As always happens when one is extra keen to get a particular buck, the harder one tries the more one fails! Roe bucks would appear for a moment and then only present their backsides. Or they would stand behind the only bush or branch in the area. Or they would just not show up at all on that particular night.

When the Fallow buck season came round I put in a lot of time making quite certain of the movements of one or two suitable to use for sampling. At last I was ready. On the chosen morning there was dense fog and my friends were unavoidably delayed on the road. But when they arrived the fog lifted. I took F., the lady, to try for one of the selected bucks. After a carefully planned stalk of the area, along the bed of a stream (I'd warned her to wear thigh boots), we came to the vantage point overlooking the ground where the buck should have been. The rest of the herd was there. But the buck had just moved into a thicket – his daytime resting place!

So I took her to a place where I knew she would find the other buck and described how to stalk the ground. It is always rather frustrating waiting for someone to stalk a deer when one cannot see what is happening. I waited an hour. Then the peace of a beautiful October morning was shattered by the most pungent language I had heard for a long while. Shortly after, this very sporting lady emerged on to the ride. She was bespattered with mud and presented a picture of glorious rage. She had spent the hour crawling very slowly down the bed of a muddy stream and at last she had got within thirty yards of the buck. Slowly she raised the rifle and squeezed the trigger – a misfire! At the second misfire the buck departed amid a volley of well-directed abuse.

The following May my friend and this lady were able to come over in the Roe buck season, as samples were required from a Roe buck. We lined out on three high seats in a row at about three hundred yards apart. A fourth rifle was to go independently into the adjoining piece of woodland which was near his house. It was pouring with rain. I wondered whether the fourth rifle would go out. Suddenly in the distance there was a great roar, followed by a volley of swear words. I was one thousand yards away, as I checked afterwards, yet the clarity of the words would have done credit to the B.B.C.; acoustics in the forest were exceptionally clear that evening! I knew he had started, and thought he must have fallen over his dog. (In fact it turned out to be his sow.) Five minutes later I heard a Roe buck barking and knew for certain that he had gone into the forest. Each of us saw Roe bucks that night – not one of us had a shot. The last rifle, walking back in the dark, was nearly run into by a buck. It came dashing up from behind, so close that he could hear the sound of its cleaves on the soft rain-washed ground. He heard its intake of breath when it stopped in amazement, within a few feet of him. Then he saw it, as a shadow, disappear.

Incidentally these investigations have now shown that lungworm gives a high measure of natural control amongst Roe deer in the New Forest. But Fallow deer do not suffer any appreciable losses, although fawns may become infected.

★   ★   ★   ★   ★

The following story was told to me by a friend, Arthur, who controls deer in Hampshire.

Late one Friday evening, a friend of his telephoned.

'Hallo, Arthur. I'm in your part of the world for the night. Any chance of shooting a buck tomorrow?'

He was rather surprised, for Harry (that is not his real name), splendid fellow though he is, had never shown any interest in any field sport, so far as he knew.

'What rifle have you got, Harry?' he asked rather guardedly.

'Oh, I'll borrow yours. It's all right, I've done a lot of shooting on the range at different times.'

Now it is quite wrong for anyone, however experienced, to use a strange rifle on deer before he has had a chance to get used to it on a target which cannot suffer if the shot is misplaced. Yet, obviously, as they would have to be out at dawn, there would be no chance for Harry to test the rifle first. Arthur thought hurriedly: he could turn him down flat. But that would disappoint him. As only Fallow bucks are in season, perhaps it would be kinder to arrange that he only saw does. He would still have the excitement of a dawn foray, and of stalking deer.

'All right, Harry, meet me at 7 a.m.'

It was just getting light when they met. Arthur took the rifle out of its slip, put in an empty cartridge and handed it to him. 'You'd better test the trigger pull, at any rate.'

He fired one or two rather hasty shots at imaginary targets (imaginary rabbits bolting across the ride, Arthur thought). 'Fine, Arthur, I can manage that.'

They set off down a grassy ride, sodden with dew. 'Ssh, Harry, not a sound now,' Arthur said, with exaggerated caution. At the end of the ride there was an earth bank. One hundred yards along the bank was a clearing with three or four turkey oaks. It so happened that these were the only oak trees in that part of the area which were bearing acorns that year. Eight Fallow does, and fawns, had been feeding on the acorns for a week. Arthur described to Harry how he should stalk the area. 'Mind, now, you may only shoot a pricket with spikes less than his ears, or a small buck. Don't shoot any does.'

'Right,' he said, and set off, rifle held at the ready. After five paces he turned and came back.

'Look, Arthur, let me get this right. I don't want to make a mistake. Does don't have horns, do they?'

As a matter of fact, antelopes and cows have horns, but male deer have antlers. 'No Harry,' Arthur replied gravely, 'make sure you only shoot one with antlers.'

Arthur sat down and had a smoke. It was at the beginning of the rut and presently he heard a buck groaning. The buck was in the opposite direction to where Harry had gone. Arthur moved down the ride and located the buck in an open stand of Norway spruce. He could not see him without showing himself and there was really no chance of getting at him because there just was no cover.

Half an hour later Harry was back. 'See anything?' Arthur asked.

'Not a damn thing, Arthur, there are no deer here!'

'Well, look, Harry, there's a buck groaning in the Norway spruce over there. Would you like to try him?'

'By Jove, yes. Where is he?' said Harry, ready to fire from the hip.

'You'll have to cross this open space and get to that single bush. From there you'll be on your own and you'll have to decide how to proceed.'

As he spoke a doe ran out from behind the bush and went away bouncing on stiff legs, tail erect showing the white warning flag, and barking.

'Bad luck, Harry, that's torn it. Never mind, you may as well go to the bush to see if you can get a glimpse of the buck. But I fear he'll have gone.'

Harry set off, crouching, rifle at the ready and finger almost on the trigger – like an exaggerated Indian in a Western.

He reached the bush, crouched down and then, looking back over his shoulder, made a sign to Arthur, which he thought meant he had seen something. A moment later Harry leapt to his feet and fired apparently into the centre of the bush without wasting time on the formality of taking aim! Arthur was astonished. Harry turned round with a triumphant smile on his face. 'It's all right, Arthur, I got him all right!'

There, ten paces from him, the other side of the bush, was a dead buck. And what a buck! His right antler consisted of a single long brow tine. The left was just a knob.

'Good lord, Harry – you've shot a unicorn! What happened?'

'Well,' he said, 'as I crept up to the bush, he was coming up the other side. I had to shoot a bit quick because he saw me and was making off.'

What had happened was that the buck had heard him, or seen some movement and, thinking it was another buck, had come up to investigate.

They had a photographing session and then started to drag out the buck. He was heavy and in good condition. By the time they'd dragged him to the car Harry's enthusiasm was waning.

'You know, Arthur, I don't think I want to do much of this deer shooting. It's really too easy, isn't it?'

The buck, when dressed out, showed that he had had a terrible road accident, having been hit by a car or possibly a lorry. All his ribs had been broken. Such is nature's amazing power of recovery that his ribs had mended, in different positions, and he had regained his full normal strength, including the ability to rut.

★   ★   ★   ★   ★

Some deer had been raiding the fields on the west of the forest, over the boundary. Among them was one buck with quite a good head, except that one antler had rather a split palm.

I knew where they would return at dawn, so I put R., a very keen stalker, whose business confines him to London, on a high seat just inside some old gnarled oak trees. If the bucks skirted the woodland where R. was, he would see them against the skyline, so I told him that he could then come off his seat and stalk them. I described the buck I wanted him to shoot, to comply with the official licence which had been issued to him.

Then I went to a high seat which overlooked the whole area. I had only been there a few minutes when I saw four deer approaching – two bucks and two prickets. One of the bucks was the one we were after.

They walked across my front at about sixty yards, heading straight for R., so, of course, I did not shoot.

It was quite exciting watching them go under the trees where I knew R. was and I waited for the sound of his shot. But a few moments later the four deer came running from under the trees. They stopped in the open and then the two bucks proceeded to fight. They were only eighty yards from R., but I knew that he could not see them, although he must hear the clash of their antlers. It was obvious that they had turned back when they came upon the scent of our footsteps where we had walked to R.'s seat.

After a while the deer skirted the edge of the wood and I knew R. could see them and do a stalk. About twenty minutes later I heard his shot. To my great disappointment he missed, although he had a very exciting stalk of the buck with the split palm.

A week later I took the son of a neighbour, who had never shot a Fallow buck, to the same area. I sat with him on R.'s seat and put Johnny on the seat I had occupied. The deer had been feeding on the neighbour's land.

This time we had not long to wait before there was a shot from Johnny (he shot a small sorel) and about two minutes later two bucks came in at rather an awkward angle. They passed behind some hollies and would have to cross an open space at any moment. The first buck was a very good one and I did not want it shot. The second was a shootable sorel.

'Take the second,' I whispered. The words were hardly out of my mouth before a whole lot more deer ran in to join the first two, and immediately deer started to cross the opening. I realised at once that number two was no longer the same buck, but at that moment there was a loud report and the buck (now number two) fell dead in his tracks.

'Have I shot the right one?' asked the youngster excitedly, as bucks dashed wildly in all directions, the biggest buck crashing right under the seat. 'Yes,' I replied, very doubtfully.

We climbed down and walked over to the dead buck. It was the same one that R. had missed the week before, shot cleanly through the neck. I was delighted and the lad was at that moment in his seventh heaven, as he stooped over the dead beast. I suddenly realised he was looking for the bullet hole near the heart and I caught a look of astonishment in his eye when he saw a neat round hole in the neck. I said nothing. That has happened to all of us at one time or another!

IX

The Great White Buck of Burley

In 1948 a sandy-coloured fawn was born in Knightwood in the New Forest. Its mother was a normal-coloured Fallow doe. During the deer shooting season she was spared, so the fawn grew up to be strong, and thrived. It was a buck fawn and the following May the little buttons on its head grew into two long spikes and its coat turned white. This white pricket was well known to the keepers. The New Forest white deer are always a deep cream or sandy colour when they are fawns and with one exception, a doe with pink eyes, their eyes are a normal colour.

Two years later another sandy fawn was born in the same area and in due course it, too, grew into a strong white pricket with two long spikes. This pricket also became well known in the area.

However, during the next year one of these two white deer disappeared and it is not known for certain which of the two survived. This is unfortunate, because the survivor became a legendary figure in the area, and it would have been nice to know exactly how old he was at the end. My own view is that it was the first one, born in 1948, which disappeared and that the Great White Buck of Burley, as he became known, was born in 1950.

I first saw him in the autumn of 1959. It was only a fleeting glimpse as he made off between the boles of large pine trees, but it was enough to arouse my keen interest. During the next three years I got to know him well. He carried a perfectly shaped head and when he was in his prime no other buck in the whole forest was his equal. It was from him that I learnt much of the movements and habits of the Fallow deer of the New Forest. He became very well known in the fields around Burley Lodge. In fact those fields were his main winter feeding ground. At times he would raid Burley Lodge garden, and other gardens, quite impartially. Some of his worst raids were on the local keeper's garden, which is protected on three sides by six foot netting, with a normal fence on the front. He would enter by jumping the gate. Then, if cornered, he would fly out over the high netting, although no Fallow would jump this in cold blood.

One night the keeper was called to the telephone. As he was talking he could hear a deer munching his garden produce on the other side of the window! As soon as he hung up, he grabbed a torch and ran out into the garden. There was the Great White Buck, with his face, forehead and mouth dripping red. The keeper was horrified to see such evidence of a terrible wound on his favourite buck – until he realised the old devil had just finished eating a whole row of beetroot, the juice of which in the torchlight looked like blood.

Each year, when he cast, we searched for his antlers. Only one was found, in the spring of 1960. I have used this antler at many lectures to illustrate the wonder of nature, which insists on a buck producing such a huge growth each year between early May and mid-August. It also illustrates the perfect 'type' of Fallow antler – broadly palmated, with a long brow tine.

One day in July, 1960, I was walking quietly along a forest ride, with my black labrador, when I saw a pair of huge antlers in velvet, in a bed of green bracken. I recognised the Great White Buck at once. What a wonderful chance for a photograph if only he would remain there while I got the camera. I hurried back to the car, left Sooty there and returned with the camera. Luck seemed to be with me as the antlers had not moved. With camera poised, I advanced slowly and at ten paces distance success seemed certain, for he was sure to jump up at any moment and show himself.

Suddenly the antlers moved round and a ripple ran through the tops of the bracken away from me. At about eighty yards distance he came into the open and stood for some ten seconds studying me. Did I imagine a smirk on his face? Then he was gone.

I was intrigued to discover how he had achieved such an invisible get-away and at first it seemed certain that he had slipped into a concealed drain. The keepers have often said that sometimes a buck will creep away on his knees, but until then it had seemed hard to believe.

But there was no drain. He had in fact crept away 'on hands and knees', so to speak, and starting from a lying position, only ten paces from me, had shown no part of his body other than his antlers! Another day I did eventually get a photograph of him as he crossed the road in Dames Slough, but it is not a good one.

That September I was after a buck with a curious deformity in one antler. I had crept up close and was waiting until he presented a killing shot, with a safe background. It was a long wait and quite suddenly the Great White Buck appeared. He came within twenty yards of me and it was obvious that he sensed that I was there, although he neither saw nor heard me and could not have winded me. He was nervous, and curious at the same time, and even after he had passed, he kept looking over his shoulder. I waited until he had gone right away before I took the buck I was after.

He had several different routes by which he would approach the fields, according to which part of the forest he used for the day-time. One such path, which he was wont to use more regularly than any other, passed under a great pollard beech tree. There is a natural platform between the great limbs, which have sprung up from the point where the tree was pollarded some three hundred years ago. On this two or more people may sit in comfort. So we placed a short ladder to this natural look-out. One has to be in position in good time, for the deer appear as shadows, when the last light is fading. Seldom do they reach this point before the cars passing along the main road put on their side-lights. By headlight time they have all passed. When the Great White Buck was with them it was very exciting, for one could pick him out in the gloaming with glasses, a hundred yards or more away. Yet, although usually he was accompanied by four or five other great bucks of normal colour, one could not see them until they were very much nearer, because they did not show up. Sometimes they passed so close

that one could almost lean down and touch their antlers, and I have heard their breathing and wondered why they did not hear mine.

On one occasion, just as I was expecting to see the deer, a fox appeared right under the tree. He was only a faint shadow and he was lost to sight, because of the bad light, before he had left the open ground. Very softly I squeaked like a rabbit, with lips pressed to the back of my hand. He was back at once and appeared to put his fore feet on to the bottom rung of the ladder while he stared up. Then he was gone with an angry whisk of his brush. At the same moment a tawny owl landed on a branch a few feet away. He, too, was astonished to see a man and not a mouse.

One still windless evening I came to this pollard tree seat in good time, knowing the deer were lying up only a couple of hundred yards away. I hoped to see them in a better light because they were so near. After I had settled down, a stiff breeze sprang up behind me. I was high enough above the ground for my scent to be above the deer, but I knew if I came down to ground level they would wind me at once.

Suddenly there was the most appalling clanging noise. The keeper's house by the main road is about a hundred and fifty yards away. Beside this is an open space where a contractor's man was now servicing a T.D.18 caterpillar tractor. It seemed that servicing was a matter of belting its most resonant parts with a sledge hammer, intermittently. The whole forest reverberated with this unnatual clamour. Although deer will become accustomed to many noises, metallic noises are the most alarming to them. Many a deer has been saved by the click of a safety catch or the light touch of field glasses against a rifle barrel.

I was furious, particularly so because I was pinned down by the ever-increasing wind from the wrong direction. I could not move to another seat. After a while the noise ceased and I began to recover my self-composure. Then it started up again and I fumed. This sequence of events continued until, during a quiet session, I saw the Great White Buck and seven other bucks quietly walking along their usual path. The light was going and I was fairly sure that the wielder of the sledge hammer would no longer be able to see the particular nut which he was tormenting. When the deer were within twenty-five yards of me, there was a resounding clang. It sounded as though the whole machine had broken to bits! Deer, when alarmed, seem just to melt away – one moment they are there and the next they are not. But the Great White

Buck and his companions, all old, experienced and wily deer, just kept on walking. Not one glanced towards this most abnormal, ear-splitting sound.

There is a simple explanation. In common with many animals, deer have the ability to pin-point sound (and the source of scent, for that matter). If we see a man, we know he is standing by a certain tree. Deer do not have to see him to know that he is standing by the tree, so long as they can hear or wind him.

In this case they knew perfectly well that the sound was coming from outside the block of woodland (their territory) in which they were, even though it was only a hundred and fifty yards away. Had it been but ten yards inside 'their' woodland, no doubt they would have fled precipitately.

In the autumn of 1960 the Great White Buck rutted in Knightwood, not very far from where he was born. After the rut he disappeared, as male deer do, but not long after he turned up on his usual winter ground. In 1961, however, we were unable to find where he rutted and he was missing for quite a while.

In 1962, therefore, I determined to try to find where he was rutting. I went out to look for him on October 18th at dawn. It was dense fog – visibility only thirty yards – when I pulled up at the inclosure gate. As soon as I got out of the car three different bucks could be heard groaning very clearly, not very far away.

A little way further a white buck walked across the ride into a block of oak. Here the fog was less dense and I recognised him at once as a six-year-old I had often seen last year. He had a nice head, rather short, but with wide even palms. A big buck was groaning some two hundred yards away. I started to stalk him. The fog was beginning to disperse and I soon saw his outline. His left antler was a nice even shape – had his right antler been the same he would have been a very good buck. But it was very much larger. Had his left antler been as large he would have been one of the very best in the forest. Presently he moved away.

Hearing another old buck groaning some way off, and knowing that he would be near a knoll of bare beech trees, I stalked this area. As I got near I heard a crashing of branches and thought that I had flushed some does. Slowly I moved through the bushes. Suddenly the bracken shook thirty yards away and the same buck, which I had already seen once, stood up. What I had heard was this buck making his bed to lie in! He stood looking at me with mingled surprise and disgust. Then he moved quietly away. There was no wind, so I started to circle back towards the car. I had not gone far when I was startled by a loud crash some distance away. It sounded like a lorry going over the cattle grid five hundred yards off, at fifty miles an hour. An intermittent clashing noise followed, like small very dry boughs being thrown into a lorry. I realised that it was two bucks fighting and guessed that the big buck I had moved had blundered into another's territory.

It did not take me long to retrace my steps. The two were in an area of open beech woodland two hundred and twenty yards from where I had first heard them. I crawled to within a hundred yards and crouched behind a tree stump. A wonderful spectacle was revealed. There were two great bucks with their antlers interlocked. The one was the buck I had already seen twice and the other was equally large-bodied; but his antlers were rather longer and much more even. As they fought, the muscles of their hind quarters and backs strained and quivered while they strove to gain ground. Beyond them, completely ignoring them, stood the Great White Buck of Burley, now miles from his own ground! Forty yards from me stood another great buck, looking over his shoulder towards the combatants. Beyond him a pricket grazed unconcerned by the battle and four younger bucks, all well-proportioned beasts, moved restlessly backwards and forwards.

The battle raged furiously. First one would gain a few yards as the hind legs of the other slithered backwards. Then the other would regain his foothold and force the first one back. Sometimes neither would give at all and their great neck muscles would stand out as they twisted this way and that, while the forest rang with the crisp clash and rattle of their antlers. At one stage they fought through a thin cover of bushes, the twigs and leaves flying in all directions. Sometimes one would twist away, while the other would rush in at his ribs or hind quarters, only to be met by an adroit turn and reclash of antlers. Gradually they moved down hill towards me, until they were within forty yards. I got out my camera and photographed them, although the light was very poor. Shortly after, one caught the other amidships and gave him a tremendous pummelling behind the shoulder. 'That will end him,' I thought. But no, he twisted round and re-engaged with another fierce crash.

I estimated that the battle had lasted twenty minutes – and I am quite certain that that was a close estimate – then suddenly it was all over. One moment they were straining as before, antlers interlocked, the next moment one of them suddenly turned and ambled off. The victor, my fine buck with the uneven head, followed slowly for sixty yards or so to make sure that the vanquished really had gone. Then he came back equally slowly. His tongue was hanging and there was froth on his nostrils and his hide was black with sweat.

In the meantime the Great White Buck was parading up and down groaning all the time and sometimes rattling a small holly with his antlers. He was accompanied by four or five does, most of whom were lying down. Very carefully I sketched his head on the back of an envelope, even though the exact shape of his antlers was already firmly fixed in my mind.

After a short rest the winner of the fight wandered, groaning and grunting, into the Great White Buck's arena. The Great White Buck came across towards him, brushing the other's rump with his own shoulder. At once the big one turned and their antlers crashed and locked. This time I timed the fight. It was over in five minutes. Two such terrific fights were too much for the one buck and the Great White Buck very easily drove him off.

Very dejectedly the vanquished buck came towards me and stood, panting, in some holly bushes not forty-five yards away, with his head drooping. Then he came through the fence and lay down quite close to me.

On the other side of me another white buck appeared. I recognised him as a good six-year-old, son of the Great White Buck. He came forward on his toes, head held high, spoiling for a fight. Without any hesitation at all he walked straight into the other's arena. Again the Great White Buck sidled up to him and pressed him with his shoulder from behind, walking almost beside him. A moment later they were locked in battle. But it was only a brush. The young buck was very quickly 'routed' by his father.

The buck lying down near me must have spotted me, because, when I turned to look for him, he had gone. He had just faded away noiselessly.

By now the mist had gone. A bright morning sun shone through the golden beech trees and lit up the carpet of brown leaves which had already fallen to the ground. The Great White Buck was still there looking magnificent against the autumn colours and the gold and russet fronds of bracken. He moved across to where the does were lying and nuzzled one to her feet. After three false attempts he served her, an event which is extremely rare for a human eye to witness. It was exactly 9.32 a.m.

For some little time after the rut was over, the Great White Buck was not seen at all. He was recuperating from the strain of the rut and the long period of fasting, for Fallow bucks eat almost nothing during the rut. Then, towards the end of November, he turned up again in his usual haunts.

Hard weather set in early, before Christmas. Before the New Year the forest was deep in snow, which lay for an unprecedented length of time. All wild life suffered severely.

At dawn on the morning of January 10th, clad in a white duffle coat, I was in Dames Slough, the Great White Buck's territory. Suddenly I saw him lying in the snow under a hazel bush. He was with his son – the one he had fought off so easily during the rut. He stood up, looking a dirty cream colour against the pure white of the snow, and stared back at me. But he did not move away and I passed on. Some weeks later I saw a fine white buck standing in the snow close to the roadside fence. Obviously he was another son, as a close and careful scrutiny of the shape of his antlers proved. The old buck was never seen again, alive.

On April 18th, 1963, his remains were found, lying close to where I had last seen him. He had been dead some time. The rigours of the winter had proved too much for the old fellow and he had had to answer nature's final call. For thirteen years he had roamed at will through this part of the forest, which would know him no more. Very sadly I examined his head and my thoughts went back to that glorious autumn morning when I had been privileged to witness his vigour and magnificence.

His antlers now have pride of place in the Verderers Hall at Lyndhurst; and, what is more important, at least three of his sons survive. The oldest one has taken over his father's territory and his antlers, like his father's, are among the best in the forest.

Nature's job of survival has been accomplished and the Great White Buck lives on.

X

Odd Sorties and Luck

The outcome of a successful sortie after deer depends, of course, on skill and knowledge, but luck plays a great part, too.

The keeper in a certain forest in Dorset had told me of a fine old Roe buck which had been doing damage to the hay fields. He wanted me to take him. I did a careful survey of the area. It was his wont to lie up for the day in a dense thicket of Scots pine and then pass through a fairly open pole crop on his way to the fields. It should have been easy to shoot him in the pole crop. I put up two simple hides, one in a ditch for morning and one in a little heap of brash for evening. For the next *two years* I tried for that buck on numerous occasions. More often than not I did not even see him. Sometimes I would obtain a fleeting glimpse of him making off. Other people saw him frequently.

July of the third year arrived and I had not been after him at all.

Then one day I had a sudden hunch to seek him out. In the case of deer, as with flighting wildfowl, it is important to take notice of 'hunches'. If one doesn't, one spends the rest of the day imagining missed opportunities. If one follows a hunch, one of three things happens: it may be a complete failure – in that case the urge is assuaged; or, more often, one gains useful knowledge for the next occasion; or it succeeds.

As soon as I got into the car at dawn I noticed that my thumb stick was missing. I had left it where I had parked the car in the heart of the New Forest the night before. I was annoyed for two reasons. I never like stalking without a thumb stick. It gives that extra measure of steadiness when taking a standing shot. Apart from that it was a very special blackthorn thumb stick.

By the time I parked the car at the end of the road it was light enough to shoot. Quietly I moved down a grassy ride in order to take up my position in the ditch. I knew it would be overgrown since last year and wondered whether it would be any good at all. I was about a hundred yards from the old hide, when suddenly there he was standing watching me. His antlers were shorter than last year's, but wide and enormously thick at the base. His heart was obscured by a small branch of brash. As I looked through the telescope in search of a hole in the brash large enough to take a bullet, the buck took a pace forward and showed the base of his neck. He never knew what hit him. He had enormously thick coronets almost fused at the centre and was altogether a most pleasing head – the more so since he was an old buck that should have been shot a year before. This all happened within five minutes of leaving the car. It was a coincidence that his path should have crossed mine just then, after two fruitless mosquito-ridden years of seeking him: luck indeed.

Later that morning, on the spur of the moment, my wife and I decided to go into Fordingbridge to buy some goldfish for our new pond. While we were walking down the main street, two hikers approached us. One of them was walking proudly along, carrying my thumb stick! He was dumbfounded when told exactly where he had found it that morning in the heart of the forest and he gave it up like a lamb. As I visit Fordingbridge only about once in five or six weeks, and as I would never have seen the lad had I been five minutes earlier, or later, it would take a computer to work out the odds of such a thing happening. That is the third time it's been lost, so I shall have to put my name and address on it.

A third coincidence happened within minutes. We walked into the pet shop and enquired about goldfish. 'Sorry, we've sold right out', we were told. At that moment the door opened and a man walked in and asked the shopkeeper: 'Do you want to buy any goldfish? I've got thirty for sale!' How often does one meet a member of the public flogging live goldfish? 'To' and 'Fro', the result of the transaction, now swim happily among the water-lilies in the pond, much to young Peter's delight.

One day a friend told me of a very old Sika stag, whose antlers were not much more than stumps. I went after him the next evening. Feeding on the ride beside the block in which he had been seen were six Sika, mostly hinds. But one, a young stag, had its right antler hanging downwards beside its face. It was not difficult to get within range, but it was a long wait before he presented a shot clear of the other deer. At the shot he leapt forward and disappeared under the trees, the other deer following in the same direction. I was sure I had shot him through the heart and that he would be dead, nearby. A bunch of 'pins' (hair cut off by the bullet) and a spot or two of 'paint' (blood) indicated that he had certainly been hit.

Normally Sooty, my black labrador, is in the car ready for such an emergency. As he hunts mute, I put a small Swiss cow-bell on to his collar; his excitement is tremendous when he hears the tinkle of that bell! However, on this occasion Silver, his sister, a yellow labrador, was with me. She is not experienced with deer, but she followed a trail for a quarter of a mile and then lost it.

Shortly after, I met the keeper. He had heard the shot and he had seen six Sika pass him, one of which had a broken antler. We searched until dark without result.

The next day with a friend and three keepers we searched the whole area. Just to make quite sure that the stag was not lying dead near where I had shot him we walked in line, twenty yards apart, through the whole block. We found nothing. We gave up at lunch time, but my friend remained to try for the old Sika, as it was he who had first seen him. He did not see this stag, but he did find mine lying dead within forty yards of where I had shot him! Goodness knows how we had missed him.

Ten days later I went in search of the old stag again. I was stalking down the ditch of the next ride, when I saw a Sika stag with his head down, feeding. When he raised his head I was astonished to see that his right antler was hanging down beside his face! By all appearances he was the same stag I had shot ten days ago. I squeezed the trigger, wondering whether I would need a silver bullet. At the shot he wheeled round and galloped straight towards me. He fell stone dead (shot through the heart) into the ditch a few yards from me. He was identical to the one already shot, and that explained how the head keeper had seen six deer, one with a broken antler, after I had shot the first.

Twelve months later to the day, the head keeper was walking down the ride where the first one was shot, when he saw again a stag with its right antler hanging down, exactly where I had shot him! After a long stalk he managed to shoot this stag, too. The three heads are as alike as any deer heads ever could be.

Until this had happened we had been somewhat worried by a number of deformities which had occurred in the Sika of this area. It was always one antler which was deformed near the coronet, often leaving only a lump. The three stags with the broken antlers gave us the reason. The only possible explanation seems to be that in this area there is a large stag (as indeed there is) who takes a delight in playing with younger stags. He has developed the knack of twisting his antlers sideways and so wrenching the right antler of the younger beast.

The following story shows the importance of seizing an opportunity as soon as it is presented.

I had never shot a Roe in Roe Wood, but there was a buck with uneven antlers which had been doing much damage and I had been after him several times. If I drove through the wood with friends to show them deer, he was always there, but if I took a rifle he never turned up.

One day a friend at the Ely Game Advisory Service invited me to lunch to meet an American, who is one of the world's top tranquilliser specialists. He had just returned from the Congo where he had been tranquillising gorillas. His job was to sit in the back of a Land Rover with a tranquillised gorilla and give it another shot of dope every time it came round. He said that after several days of this treatment it became quite good-natured, but when I said I would like to give him a list of people who weren't good-natured, he said everyone had tried that one on him!

He was a very nice chap and as he was anxious to see some deer I took him out in the forest. We had to stop at a filling station for petrol. He pricked up his ears at my order: 'Say, what did you say? *Two* gallons of gasoline? What are you trying to do – wean it?'

On the way to look at a herd of Fallow deer we passed through Roe Wood. Sure enough there was the Roe buck feeding in an open glade below the road. We watched him for a while and then drove on and found the Fallow deer. My American friend was able to photograph them from the car and he was delighted. On the way back I told him that the Roe buck was one I had been after many times.

'Say, why don't you shoot him right now?' he asked.

'He's sure to have moved,' I replied.

But as we drove back, to my surprise, the buck was still there.

'Stop the auto and shoot him,' said the tranquillising expert.

By chance the buck was standing where it was a safe shot. But no self-respecting Roe will allow one to get out of a car in full view and shoot it, and I said just that.

'Well, there he is. You sure should shoot him.'

I got out of the car, took out my rifle, loaded it, and stepped to the side of the road in full view of the buck. For some extraordinary reason he did not move.

'Say, that was some shot! Two hundred yards and stone dead. I'll sure tell the guys back home about that.'

Now I have a rule that we do not shoot at over one hundred yards. So I was not exactly flattered. A fluky shot at two to three hundred yards may be very pleasing if it comes off – but the risk of wounding is too great. To my way of thinking, a rifle should never be fired unless there is a certainty of putting the bullet in the right place. That is one of the main differences between shotgun shooting and rifle shooting.

You put up a shotgun and fire and you may well expect to kill – but it may not happen, even with the expert.

With a rifle, if you do not take long shots, you come up steady on the target, squeeze the trigger and the bullet must go precisely where it is aimed. The point is that if you are not holding steady – and a 'scope shows that – you must not squeeze the trigger. Pause and try again.

'Oh, it wasn't quite that far. It's hardly eighty yards,' I said.

'It was every yard of two hundred yards and no mistake.'

We went up to the buck. Apart from an uneven head, it had an extra tine behind its ear, in a peculiar position. I had not seen this because the ear concealed it, but being interested in freaks I was quite pleased. The buck and I were photographed all ends up. Then I proceeded to drag out the buck. The American hung back and did not offer to help, but after a few moments he came striding up. He had been pacing the distance.

'You were quite right – seventy-five yards,' he said. 'But it was still some shot – it was a mighty little buck!'

My American friend told me this story of American hunters. 'I was sitting in a coffee bar when in came two hunters, rifles over their shoulders. "Did you see a deer?" said one. "No," replied the other, "but I had two shots at the sound of one"!'

★　　★　　★　　★　　★

When one is alone the difficulty of dragging out a big buck and loading it is often quite a problem. I have a roof rack on the car and I tie the antlers with a rope and pull to get the head and fore legs up towards the rack. Then I tie the rope so that it supports the weight of the fore part of the deer. It is a simple matter to lift and swing the haunches into the shooting brake, release the rope and slide the front end in. One day I had shot a huge Sika stag. Puffing and perspiring all the way I had dragged it, a yard at a time, until I reached a road to which I could bring the car. Then, by the method described, I loaded the stag and delivered him to the keeper. A few days later I met the forester.

'I believe you shot a Sika the other day,' he said.

'Yes, I suppose you saw blood on the road where I loaded him.'

'No,' he answered, 'one of my men told me he saw you striding through the forest with a great stag across your shoulders!' Which shows how legends start!

Luck is a fickle mistress. It doesn't do to jilt her. One day my wife wanted to buy some venison for a special purpose – a sort of fête she was organising to collect funds for our local church repairs.

As I drove through the forest the sun came up like a baleful yellow ball. I had never before seen quite such a menacing sky. It seemed to augur ill luck for the morning's outing.

However, as soon as I started to stalk I came across a herd of sixteen Red deer returning from their night's feeding.

The big stag had been cast for a good while. Last year, just about the time of the rut, he had been knocked down by a car on the main road and given up for dead. But he had recovered in the miraculous way which animals do from ghastly injuries, although he had been lame all through the winter. So we were all very anxious to see what effect the accident had had on his new antlers. It was now May 15th and I was pleased to be able to get a good view of his head. The new growth was up about four inches and at this stage appeared perfectly normal. (When he was clean we found that his left bey tine was missing – the only after effect.) There were two brockets with him; one had not cast, but the other had lost one of his spikes.

Further on I saw a shootable Roe buck walk into a thicket. I knew that he would pass through the thicket and come out onto an open area. All I had to do was to make a detour and stalk quietly down the bed of the stream until I came to the open glade. This I did with no difficulty, but to my surprise there was no sign of the buck. Then suddenly I saw him right in the middle of the clearing, not forty yards away. How I had missed seeing him at first glance I don't know. Fortune was smiling on me, for he had not seen me at all, and there he was, broadside on, as easy a shot as possible. I watched him quietly grazing, frequently lifting his head, as an old buck will, to look for danger.

He had a fine head. I remembered that I had let him off several times last year and he was almost an old friend. The church repair fund did not seem to be quite so important as it had been when I left home. I could not bring myself to shoot him.

Completely unconscious of the danger he had just been in, he walked past me twenty-five yards away. Then he paused and stretching his neck to the fullest extent, reached up to pluck five fresh green beech leaves in quick succession. He wandered on, circling somewhat to the left until he stood upon the bank of the stream. I was now fully exposed to his view as he looked down stream. I could see the surprise in his eyes as he saw me standing there. He left the stream, barked, ran a few yards and then stood behind a tree motionless. So often a Roe will do that, making the most of any available cover while he watches silently. At such moments he is more curious than alarmed and if he has barked, an answering bark from the stalker will frequently bring him a step forward into the open. Not wishing to deceive him, I took off my hat and waved it gently at him. He made off with disgruntled coughs.

Further on I came across a white Fallow doe with two other does and watched them for a while. Beyond them was an entrancing pink cloud among the spring greenness. It was crab apple, the blossoms combining innocence with satisfying beauty. It would last another week. But never would it look more lovely than in the early light of that spring morning.

A bird flew across my path and caught my eye at once. It settled on a branch and at quite close range the glasses showed up every detail of its plumage and its huge beak. It was a hawfinch, a bird that always thrills me and one which I do not see very often, because it is a rare bird.

Remembering the church venison I returned to the car and moved to another area where I knew there was a Roe buck. I stalked very slowly through the area and came up to four Fallow, one after the other. Then I realised that I had lost my chance for the day, having spurned my earlier buck. I returned towards the car and, of course, at that moment flushed the Roe buck. He had fed towards the car and had been grazing in a little glade only sixty yards away. Sooty could have shot him quite easily from the car! On the way home the road was covered with a pale green carpet of elm seed. This is the first seed of any tree to ripen and fall. If it is to germinate it must be collected and sown within twenty-four hours.

At noon the baleful sun had gone. Torrential rain fell until nine-thirty that evening and the whole forest was awash. As for the church venison – I went out morning and evening for several days, becoming more and more desperate. On the very last morning before the fête I stalked a suitable buck. Then, just as I was about to take him, he walked away giving me no chance at all. He walked through the fence into a thick patch of scrub and I despaired, but to my surprise he came out of the scrub on the other side, turned and walked back. In a matter of moments a hopeless situation became a success and venison reached the fridge in time to save the day and, I hope, the church!

On another occasion Johnny and I got up early and took up our positions before daylight on two deer seats. These seats were about five hundred yards apart and some half mile back from the fields where

I knew many deer were feeding. It seemed a certainty. Three poor bucks and three or four does should have come past Johnny's seat and half-a-dozen small deer past mine. However, neither of us saw a deer. When I climbed down I decided to try to find where the deer were. I had not gone far before I heard something in the undergrowth. An alsatian and a black retriever burst out. It was obvious that they had been hunting deer all morning and had disturbed all the deer in the area. Our luck was out.

On the way home I remembered there were often deer moving late in the morning in a certain triangular shaped oak wood.

'You stalk through it, Johnny,' I said, 'and I'll go to the south-east corner and head it off. I know the deer paths there.'

I was just creeping to the fallen log where I intended to wait when I saw a fawn in very poor condition. It was obviously one which had lost its mother early and therefore it was doing badly and ought to be shot.

It was easy to stalk within range and as the deer was in a hollow it was a perfectly safe shot. Yet I hesitated because I knew Johnny was more or less directly beyond. A shot rang out and I realised at once that Johnny was well to one side. At his shot my deer had hardly raised its head to listen before my bullet killed it instantly. A moment later I saw a small herd of deer, those disturbed by Johnny, crossing my front towards the south-west corner of the wood. I moved quickly and took up a new position, and within a matter of moments four deer came forward and stood about a hundred yards away. They were not in a safe position to shoot, and I was sure that when they moved on they would get my wind, so I was not hopeful. Presently they ran out of sight – and then reappeared about sixty yards behind me.

It often happens that an unexpected eddy of wind gives one's position away and all is lost. In this case, although my wind seemed to be blowing directly to them, some eddy must have taken my scent around them. To my surprise they were quite unaware of my presence. But a rifle shot was impossible because they were partly masked by a trailing beech branch. The glasses revealed three does and a very poor pricket. I wanted to take the pricket. No sooner had I decided this than he stepped forward clear of the branches. There was a safe background. At my shot he moved a few paces and fell dead. The others fled, but paused after running fifty yards. Another quick aim and the last in line fell without a kick.

When Johnny came up I found he had shot his beast. So in a period of time shorter than it takes to tell the story we had bagged four deer. Ten haunches were required for the Verderers' Court the following Monday, and we had obtained eight of them. Our luck had changed full circle from the complete blank at the time when we had expected success.

The story of the Verderers' haunches is of interest. By very ancient tradition the Verderers of the New Forest were allowed to course and take such deer as they met on their way to and from the Court. However, this privilege was cancelled long ago because it was realised that either the deer or the Verderers (it is not now known which) ran too fast. Nowadays, instead, once a year, each Verderer is given a haunch. (Actually it used to be a whole buck, but it has been whittled down, over the years, to a haunch.)

The evening of the same day I decided to flight a certain pond in the forest, while Johnny went to another outside the forest. Just as deer and all other animals, including man, leave their spoor, or tracks, so ducks leave the signs of their visits. Upon arrival I made a careful search for feathers. A few gulls' and two swans' feathers floated at the edge. Beyond these were many grey feathers. I waded out and collected one. What a thrill! It was a goose's breast feather. A very large number of whitefronts (for there are no other grey geese in this region) had been on the pool the night before.

There was no cover at all, but I knew that they would come very late in a bad light. The ground was too wet to take up a lying position, so I made a thin screen of two small branches and sat on my game bag on a tiny tussock, Sooty lying between my legs. An hour later I heard the wild clamour of geese in the distance, very faintly. At that moment two mallard swung in front of me. The geese were still a mile away up wind. I made a quick decision and the nearest mallard fell with a splash on to the pool. I put a $2\frac{3}{4}''$ No 4 in the empty right chamber and replaced small shot in the left with B.B. Then I tried to crouch like a hare on my tussock.

The geese appeared in three long lines. There were about three hundred of them and the whole air was ringing with their thrilling

merry music. When they were two hundred yards away they set their wings and planed down. But I judged they were still too high. They swept around in a huge clamorous mass and I could tell from the call notes that the leading skein had seen me as an object. Always wary, they circled, doubtful, not yet recognising the shape of a man. Then a small skein of a dozen took a wide sweep and, unaware of danger, crossed over the centre of the pool. The nearest goose crumpled like a stone and fell with a great splash. My second shot missed.

A few moments later all was silence again and it was difficult to believe that three hundred geese had come to this small pool. Without any doubt at all, a goose is the rarest quarry ever to be shot in the New Forest. One way and another it had been a lucky day.

*   *   *   *   *

At last I have had luck of a different sort – the fulfilment of a long search for a rubber toy.

Some years ago a friend's small boy was given a toy kangaroo with a squeak exactly like a Sika call. During the rut this toy call has been most effective in bringing Sika stags to my friend. So ever since then

I have been squeezing toys all over the country to find one! Not long ago, having a few moments to spare, when on my way to a high-powered County Council meeting, I decided to continue my search at Woolworth's. The very first toy I 'squoze' was exactly right – a rubber clown with a perfect Sika squeak. Delighted, I bought it. All through the rather dull meeting I kept fingering the rubber clown in my pocket, wondering whether the note was really right. At last I could no longer resist giving it a very gentle squeeze. The piercing Sika scream which it let out set everyone by the ears!

Now I can scarcely wait for the next rut. Meanwhile, the rubber clown is a prize exhibit among my deer trophies. In the end I gralloched the clown in order to extract his whistle. A day or two later I found the office messenger fingering the now empty clown. 'How do you get that squeak out of this here?' he enquired. 'I can't make it whistle at all!'

One evening I was stalking through woodland where I had permission to look for a Roe buck. Suddenly I heard one bark on a heavily wooded slope. He was travelling from right to left, so I hurried to the end of the next ride and stood still. A moment later a buck stepped out on to the ride at the far end. I studied him with the glasses, but had not made up my mind about him before he crossed the ride and disappeared. I hurried along to the next ride junction and stepped out very quietly, concentrating my attention on the point where I expected the buck to appear. With considerable surprise I realised that I had stopped only a couple of paces behind two men who were also standing looking down the ride. They were obviously trespassers and they had no business to be there at all. I was wearing green thigh boots (because, if necessary, it is easy to crawl in them), a camouflaged jacket, a wide-brimmed dark green hat and a mask completely obscuring my face.

In my left hand was a long thumb stick; in my right a loaded 7 mm. rifle. The two men must have sensed my presence before I had decided how to deal with the situation. They half turned and came face to face with me at no distance at all. For half a second they were paralysed with fright. Then they both let out a squeal of terror and took off down the ride, jinking from side to side as hard-pressed hares will do. After thirty yards or so the one dived into the bushes on the right and the other into the undergrowth on the left. From then on their progress could only be estimated by the crashing of branches. It was quite clear that they followed no path.

I was as surprised at their reaction as they were at my appearance. I gave them a few minutes to get out of my way, and then set off quietly continuing my reconnaissance in another direction. I came to another cross rides and peeped out. There were the two ruffians holding a confab, some fifty yards away. I stepped out into their line of sight. They whirled on their heels and took off up the ride, through the fence at the end and away across the open countryside at a pace which would have done credit to an Olympic runner. If only I had had the presence of mind to shout at them they would probably still be running.

The next night I was in another wood. I knew exactly where a very old Roe buck was wont to come out. I intended to sit behind a log and wait for him. I spent a good deal of time on a slow and careful approach and at last settled myself down behind the log, pleased with my skill in getting there so quietly. I had scarcely sat down before the buck barked and went bouncing away through the under-growth. He had been standing watching me all the time!

I knew the evening was wasted, but sat on for half an hour or so enjoying the peaceful surroundings. The log was close to a little brook and a grey wagtail ran along the bank flirting his tail and catching insects. Without doubt his mate was on a nest nearby.

Presently, in the distance, I heard a car engine being revved. Brr, Brr, Brr, Brr. It went on and on for some time. 'Some silly ass has got bogged,' I thought. So when I left I drove out by the gate nearest the unfortunate motorist.

Sure enough, by the gate was a youth, with a beautiful blonde, who looked extremely angry.

'Can you tell me where the nearest garage is, please?' he asked.

'Yes,' I replied 'that's easy, there just isn't one.'

'My car's stuck,' the youth announced rather lamely, while the blonde tried to look very helpless.

'Yes, I heard it,' I replied.

The car was a Mini-Minor. In the back was a portable radio and a lot of sweet papers. It had been backed into a secluded corner. The secluded corner happened to be a bog. It wasn't a bad bog, but the lad had lost his head and by revving up the engine had sawmilled the wheels well into the mud. I don't enjoy pushing stuck cars, so I asked if he would mind if I took the wheel while he pushed. By taking the Mini-Minor steadily she came out quite easily – better than I expected. I drove it on to the firm ground beside my own car and then got into mine.

'You'll be all right now?' I enquired rather unnecessarily.

Before I could drive off the youth thrust a pound note on to my lap through the window and disappeared. I could not have done less to earn it. I used the money to purchase a blonde rhododendron called Goldsworth Yellow. My blonde has been very accommodating and given me much pleasure every spring since then.

XI

First Stag

Every sportsman remembers the major milestones in his shooting career. As a small boy it may have been his first rabbit or his first squirrel. Later, his first snipe or woodcock, his first mallard or cock pheasant, and at last, perhaps, his first goose. All are precious records in his game book.

I have always wanted to stalk a stag. Roe and Fallow and even Sika, I had successfully achieved, long years ago. But never had there been a chance to stalk a stag.

So when Ken MacArthur, that great expert in the ways of deer, invited me to spend a couple of days in his Forest I accepted with much delight.

He and his wife Sallie met me off the sleeper at Dumfries on October 15th. As we crossed the head waters of the loch at first light, two large flights of mallard passed over the car – a good omen.

At last we turned off the public road and began a long climb through new Forestry Commission plantations. Three greyhens, who were consorting with a single cock grouse, flew across the road almost under the bonnet of the car. The cock grouse settled again in a few yards and started crowing and chuckling to himself – a glorious welcome to the hills of Scotland. Further on two Roe does scampered away; they were already in their full winter coat.

As we entered the Glen it was drizzling, but not enough to detract from the grandeur of the scene. A loch lay gleaming silver in a shallow basin surrounded by magnificent hills, with mile upon mile of brown bog beyond. A large animal was moving across one of the raised peat bogs, a mile away.

'Have you any horses in the Glen?' I asked.

'There's nae horses hereaboots,' was Ken's reply.

That was my first view of a Galloway stag. Glasses were soon focused. He was a 'muckle' hart indeed, with dark shaggy mane and black from wallowing. As he stood smelling the ground he looked as big as a buffalo.

Some way further on another fine stag appeared, walking parallel to the road little more than a rifle shot away.

'Yon's the "House Stag",' said Ken. 'Sallie sees him from the kitchen window. He's a nine-pointer.'

Soon we were carrying suitcases across the hundred yards of bog which separates the little croft from the road. One room is always left open to shelter hikers. The other downstairs room is snug and warm. There is no other house within six miles and the nearest public road is nine miles away. Truly it is a haven after the wind and rain of the hill, while the sound of a bubbling burn is always in the ears of those who rest therein.

'Back Hill of the Bush' is a legendary name which goes back through the centuries to the day when the great bogs were forests of rowan, birch and sallow. Its cheerful hearth burns the roots and stumps of those trees which the forestry ploughs have turned up and wrenched from their peaty resting place of a thousand years and more ago.

After an enormous breakfast we set off down the Glen again to test my rifle on a target, a very necessary operation. It was shooting two inches high – not a bad fault.

Ken knows every stag in the Glen. He showed me where there should

be a good young ten-pointer accompanying a single hind and calf, and
sure enough there they were. On the hillside opposite was a great beast,
an old ten-pointer who ruts in this place every year. This was the last
stag which Balfour Brown saw before he died, though he was particular
in his use of correct terms and would have known this beast as a 'muckle
hart' – for, strictly speaking, a 'stag' is a younger beast, not fit to be
shot; few sportsmen use the correct terms today.

Returning to Back Hill of the Bush we glassed the high slopes under
Craig Eazle, slopes which showed a glorious mingling of browns, fawns
and yellows, for the deer grass and the purple moor grass had already
turned to their winter shades. Close under the new forestry sheep fence
was another great stag accompanied by six or seven hinds.

'Aye, he's shootable. You can stalk him presently,' said Ken.

The clouds had lifted and the drizzle ceased, so for the first time I
could see the whole valley. What a glorious sight! On the left the tawny
boulder-strewn slopes below Craig Eazle rolled down to the brown
peat bogs of the valley bottom. To the right Craignaw, Wolf's
Slock and Dungeon, great black rocky heather-clad slopes, rising to
precipices, framed the Glen. Down the centre ran the main burn,
Cooran Lane, its banks green with fresh grass growing on the spoil of
countless spates. Here the Red deer feed at night and under the great
black precipices the huge Galloway stags roar all day. A farmer's lad,
stranger to the Glen, hearing them roaring for the first time remonstrated
with Ken. 'Yon's nae a place to keep cattle. They wouldna be finding
a bite at a'.' He had mistaken the roaring of the stags for the bellowing
of hungry cattle!

Presently Ken, Peter and myself set off to climb the lower slopes
which led to the stag I was to stalk. Peter, a stalker from an adjoining
forest, had brought over his pony, Danny. Danny is twenty years old,
good natured, very intelligent and rather greedy. He will cheerfully
bring down one stag from the hill, negotiating his way around boulders
and treading carefully over bogs. But he takes a very poor view of
having to return for a second stag on the same day – it cuts down his
eating time. Curiously enough he is the exact colour of a stag.

At length we reached a point from which we had to proceed very
carefully. At the same time the mist came down and it began to rain.
Ken led the way forward until we came to an open hollow with a small

heather-clad ridge beyond, which was half hidden in mist. We had to reach its crest before we could hope to see the stag.

Deer's eyes are better able to see through mist than man's. Therefore if there had been a hind on our side of the ridge, she would have seen us crossing the open ground; yet it would have been impossible for us to see her.

We were about to start when the mist thinned a little, and a faint shape became visible against the skyline. A hind was coming over the ridge, followed by two more. We were securely 'pinned down'. Presently the mist lifted and we could then see them clearly, well down the side of the slope. I could not help but marvel at their wonderful protective colouring. When they were grazing over the brown dwarf mountain rush, or the tawny deer grass, they just disappeared.

There was nothing for it but to crawl back out of sight of the hinds and make a detour. At this stage Ken allowed me the great privilege of completing the stalk on my own. The first eighty yard stretch was easy, as the route lay under the side of a dark peat hag. The rain was now lashing down and the mist was thicker than ever, in spite of half a gale, but the stag was grumbling and making a sort of roar, which gave some guidance. At last I reached the lower end of the same ridge where the hinds were and peeped over, but could see nothing. After a while I made out the shape of the stag, a faint blur in the mist. In ordinary daylight he would have been a reasonable shot, but under these conditions it was very chancy. It also seemed probable that he would advance towards the hinds on the same ridge, thus giving a closer shot. But the great beast was suspicious and presently he moved away and disappeared into the mist, although by sound he was only just out of my sight.

At this stage Ken joined me.

'Do you think there's any chance of crawling across the open ground in front without being seen, Ken?'

'Not much,' was his reply. However, there seemed no point in staying where I was. 'I think I'll have a go,' I said.

I am no longer quite the ideal shape for crawling, and it is a form of locomotion which has never commended itself to me. Nor am I one of those hearty individuals who welcomes the unpleasantness of being soaked from above by good honest rain, and from below by bad smelling

black peat water. However, at this particular moment I was so excited that I was oblivious to such things. As I crawled forward I felt ridiculously inadequate, for I knew that Ken's experienced eye was watching from behind, while I felt quite certain that the stag was watching from in front, especially as he was now ominously silent. I was helped to some extent by the furrows recently ploughed by the Forestry Commission and planted last winter with small Sitka spruce. But at first I had to traverse these furrows and I could not help wondering which projected the most – my tummy downwards or my bottom upwards.

Every detail of that crawl is embedded in my memory. Here a bunch of tiny heather seedlings, there a drowned spider in a small pool of rainwater an inch from my nose. At length I reached the comparative shelter of a patch of rushes and I crawled through two 'beds' where hinds had been lying that day. The mist had now closed in again. In fact, Ken said afterwards that it was so thick that I had disappeared in twenty yards. I believed I was in dead ground, but not being able to see far I was not certain. However, the furrows were now running in the right direction, more or less, and I was able to crawl up one.

Just then the stag roared again straight ahead – that was very exciting. In front of me a small flat shelf appeared and suddenly I was aware of the shape of a beast at the other side. In the mist it looked huge and I was sure it was the stag standing broadside on. Then I realised it was feeding, and my hopes fell, for a stag does not feed when roaring. Sure enough presently it raised its head – a hind. I crawled back a little way and then advanced slightly to the right. I found that I was in the centre of a small semi-circle of six hinds, each one of which presented an easy shot at forty yards. Beyond that all was hidden by the mist.

Suddenly the stag appeared as a very faint shadow beyond the furthest hind. I looked through the telescope, but it only magnified the mist particles. I couldn't even see the hind. Then the stag disappeared again.

It was now a matter of chance whether the stag would reappear before one of the hinds grazed towards me and discovered my presence.

At last he roared again to the left. Soon he emerged at the edge of the mist. It was some moments before I could decide whether he was coming towards me or moving directly away. Then he turned and stood broadside. This was it. Slowly I raised the rifle. I could just see his outline faintly in the 'scope. I held steady and squeezed. At the shot he leapt forward and then stood. I had missed! Then he moved across my front at that steady loping gait which is so typical of Red deer. All I could see through the 'scope were rain drops on the grass in front. I raised myself to my knees, found him in the 'scope and swung with him holding steady on his heart. He collapsed in a heap, the bullet having found that vital spot just above the heart.

He was an old stag with a wild sort of head – an eight-pointer. Ken and Peter soon arrived. They were chilled to the bone, but I was hot – with excitement. It had been the most thrilling experience of any I had ever had with deer.

We were all soaked to the skin, but I had a slight advantage. I had broken tradition by wearing a light pair of thigh boots and although the water was slowly percolating downwards, at least my socks were dry at the end of the day!

*　　*　　*　　*　　*

Peter is a splendid stalker, having been trained by Ken. On another occasion we found a staggie still in velvet at the end of the stag season. The staggie was with a small group of hinds on a large open flat. There was an easy approach to the flat up the wee burn which tumbled out of the centre of it. But getting to the burn was the problem. It meant a long approach from the side – upwind, of course. Ken sent Peter with me. A single hind and calf were lying on a knoll from where it seemed they could see all. But we found that by keeping right under the knoll we were in dead ground, and we got past safely and quietly. Then our troubles really started. Two hinds had been feeding down hill until they were right in our path at the point where we hoped to get into the burn. It seemed hopeless to continue, but Peter was undaunted. We crawled forward until we were within fifty to sixty yards of the two hinds, which had been joined by a knobber and another hind and calf. They had seen some movement and were suspicious, or at any rate inquisitive. With mincing steps several of them started moving towards us.

We were crouched down flat in molinia grass about twelve inches high. It seemed impossible that they would not see us. One hind and her calf continued towards us.

When a partridge or other wild animal crouches tightly pressed into the ground it may be assumed that first it disposes its limbs into a reasonably comfortable posture. In the case of a man not very accustomed to crawling about on his tummy anyway, this is not so easy. I was 'frozen' with one knee bent under me and my head screwed round in a very awkward posture. I didn't dare move anything other than my eyes.

The hind and calf came on until they were level with us, and then they stood stock still sensing danger, but not knowing where it was. They were well within twenty yards of us. In woodland, where cover is more plentiful, I have often been within twenty yards of Fallow and Roe deer, but on the open hill, with Red deer, it seems very close indeed, and an old hind is a very alert creature. I had been without food since morning and now it was nearly dusk, and at this particular moment my tummy started to rumble – no doubt in combined protest at its state of emptiness and the unaccustomed position into which it was being forced! The hind heard the sound at once, but she could not locate it. Her ears twitched. With one foot daintily raised she wrinkled her nose, testing the wind. Then she put her foot down and moved two paces forward, only to be brought to an immediate halt by another earth-shaking tummy rumble. Out of the corner of my eye I thought I could see Peter's shoulders shaking. It was touch and go whether I could control my own laughter. Maybe the hind thought it was her tummy. At any rate she passed on, taking her calf with her. We breathed again, and I was able to relax slightly and ease my uncomfortable posture.

The knobber and the other two hinds passed more quickly, a few yards farther from us, and soon all were behind a knoll, so that we could continue the stalk.

The light was fading as we gained the burn where there was good cover. I went ahead and soon reached a huge boulder. Not far the other side was a group of hinds, suspicious. I couldn't see the staggie. Then I picked him up in the gloaming light standing broadside on about a hundred and twenty yards away. Our stalk was over.

It was interesting to find that he had a grossly enlarged spleen and that, no doubt, was the cause of his failing to clean his velvet.

XII

The Ravens

The morning after my first stag, the wind had dropped and the mist had rolled back from the top of the Dungeon. It looked like being a fine day. It proved to be the most wonderful day.

The plan was to climb the high ridge leading up to Corserine, a hill of 2,668 feet, and spy for deer in the sheltered corrie on the east side. We were accompanied by Ken's two retrievers, Susie and Meg, mother and daughter, two lovely dogs who never leave his heel – at least not until a shot is fired, when Meg sometimes falls from grace!

As we started the long walk to the foot of the slope a young stag with a small parcel of hinds got our wind and made off for a mile in full view. Red deer do not take long to cover great distances. At length we reached the foot of the steep slope leading up to the 2,000 foot ridge. A raven appeared flying along the crest of the ridge, and then another. Soon we had seen nine.

The raven is the stalker's friend. Superstition has it that if a raven croaks at the start of the stalk all will be successful. If not, there is many a stalker who would not set out at all! Ravens are highly intelligent birds and, of course, they make short work of a gralloch. There is little doubt that they connect a stalker with a meal resulting from his kill, and there are many who believe that the raven attempts to direct the stalker to his quarry.

Anyway nine ravens were rather too many to anticipate a kill, and it was obvious that they had risen from a dead animal somewhere over the top of the hill.

'I hope it isn't your old sixteen-pointer,' I said. For Ken's best stag, a magnificent sixteen-pointer, normally rutted near the top of the hill.

A little while later a huge bird appeared flying high above the head of the Glen. The glasses revealed a golden eagle, and then a second came in sight. These two noble birds wheeled in vast sweeps around each other, using the upward air currents with widespread, motionless wings. With no effort at all they travelled across a mile of sky in a few moments.

At this same time our ears were filled with the sound of roaring stags, a wonderful wild sound which echoed up the Glen from so far away that strong glasses could not pick out the beasts themselves. The crisp mountain air was like champagne and, turning about, the view down the Glen was breathtaking. Through openings in the clouds, rays of sunlight lit up Loch Dee, six miles away, and then chased each other across the flanks of the Glen, lighting up the colours of the grasses and turning them tawny brown and amber. Opposite, shafts of sunlight played on the black rock faces of the Dungeon, sometimes gleaming silver as the light was reflected from smooth wet rock faces. In the distance, ten miles away or more, odd-shaped cloud patterns played above the dark mountains of Galloway.

Far away below us, no more than the size of the head of a pin, was the Back Hill of the Bush, with the road like a thread of grey cotton winding past. To our left were the slopes below Craig Eazle, where I had shot my stag of the day before. Every detail of the stalk could be followed with glasses. The handkerchief tied to the antler of the dead beast could be seen fluttering in the wind. Danny and Peter were on their way to fetch him down from the hill.

Such vast expanses of wild scenery, such incomparable and ever-changing views, such high places – they uplift and humble a man at one and the same time.

Some way up the slope of the mountain we came upon the shattered rusty engine, and other parts, of an aeroplane – a wartime casualty. Some years ago Ken had crawled up to the engine and waited, hidden behind it, until the stag he was after had walked within shot.

Ken told me the story of a German plane which crashed in this wild country during the war. So isolated is this region that the blackout had never been heard of, nor needed, and the young German pilot, having landed safely by parachute, made for a light which was the only croft in the area. An old shepherd opened the door.

'Come in, laddie,' he said, 'and make yersel at hame!'

The German could speak a little English, but could not understand a word when it was well laced with a broad Scottish accent. The next morning the shepherd and the German walked down from the hill. On the way they passed the local army unit searching for the German pilot. Because he was walking with the shepherd the German was not noticed at all and the shepherd, his eyes twinkling, said nothing. Probably the army unit was made up of Sassenachs!

Further on they met a perspiring police officer. 'You'll be takin' care of this laddie the noo,' said the shepherd.

The police officer drew his revolver and marched the very frightened German pilot down to the village, and thereby won a medal.

At last we were on the ridge 2,000 feet above sea level. Here grow the two stagshorn mosses, and the red-berried crowberry.

The view to the north and east was as fine as that to the south and west – mile upon mile of vast rolling bogs and distant lochs. In the far distance was the Star forest and Loch Doon, fed by a winding, rather sluggish river known as the Gala Lane. (In these parts the burns are known as lanes.)

Below us the ravens rose, croaking – twelve in all. We soon discovered the carcass of a sheep upon which they and the eagles, earlier, had been feeding. But the corrie held only two hinds in one place and, further on, a hind and a calf. There were no stags.

We worked our way around the shoulder of the hill keeping high up on the flank of Craig Tarson, but there was not a deer to be seen. Suddenly a shot rang out from over the march. We glassed the rock-strewn precipitous face of Mullwharchar on the other side of the Glen. In one place we found a stag and his three hinds and there were other parties of deer in several places all looking no larger than mice. Another shot, and then two more almost together – in all six shots. The stag disappeared. Whether or not he had been shot we could not make out, but this episode was to alter the whole course of our day.

When one stands high up on these hills looking across the vast expanses of bog, the main deer trails are as obvious as paths marked upon a map. There were several strong trails running from the shelter of rocky Mullwharchar, crossing the march and the bog, and then dividing for Craig Tarson and Hunt Ha'.

The shooting had evidently disturbed a good many deer. First two stags and three hinds appeared, frequently pausing to look over their shoulders. Then came a whole parcel of hinds, spread out rather like sheep, while a huge hart moved parallel to them. Viewed from above every movement was plain to see. It was most exciting to watch all these deer coming into our ground from over the march.

Of the first two stags, one was a youngster. But the other was a pretty ten-pointer. He was not one that belonged on our side. When he came to a small burn he sniffed the ground carefully and then knelt down to wallow. Soon he was crouched down full length in the wallow, but he did not roll at all.

We were on the top side of a small precipice or very steep slope. The stag and three hinds were making for the ground immediately below this slope. By retreating from the edge we were able to keep level with them, but out of sight. Ken kindly suggested that I should take this stag.

There was a little rocky promontory and I crept down a very steep incline beside it. Peeping over the edge I could see the hinds and a brocket, but I could not find the stag. At last, by leaning forward, I found him standing broadside on right under the cliff below me. It was a very easy shot and I raised the rifle. In order to bring the muzzle to bear over the edge of the rock face, however, I had to stand on tiptoe – an awkward stance, especially as I was on the edge of the precipice. Obviously there was plenty of time, so I changed my stance so as to be more comfortable. At that moment the stag turned round and started to walk towards the brocket, lengthening the distance from me at every step. As he was moving evenly, still broadside on, he was still an easy target. My shot went off a fraction of a second before I was ready – I had not realised that my finger was numb with cold. Of course I missed.

Over anxious to retrieve the situation, I fired another shot too hurriedly and missed again – a shocking performance! The stag was now moving at a very oblique angle, but I could see his right shoulder. Steadying myself I took careful aim and he humped forward. I realised that I had only wounded him. The beauty of the day faded and I cursed myself for being so grossly inefficient.

Fortunately we were able to keep the stag in sight until he disappeared under a slight ridge. He did not reappear. It was Ken's sharp eyes which spotted the tip of an antler. He was lying under a small group of large boulders. We approached him very cautiously, and a few moments later he had been despatched.

It is a curious fact that during the rut a stag secretes much adrenalin, and as a result he is able to withstand a wound which at other times would prove fatal. He also bleeds much less freely. There is no doubt that outside the rut the first hit should have brought down my stag.

After the gralloch we dragged him to a path ready for Danny's attention and then proceeded on our way below Craig Tarson. It was then that Ken told me that at the time of my shot he was watching two enormous stags fighting. Of course, the shot broke it up.

We found the one hart, a really huge beast with tremendous thick wide antlers, together with a royal and a young stag and a parcel of hinds in Hunt Ha'. It was obviously going to be a very awkward stalk for Ken, but as he started, a pair of ravens came over the hill and flew croaking over the deer. I knew the stalk would not fail.

I sat on a rock with the dogs – Meg tied to the strap of my thigh boots and Susan sitting as good as gold beside her. I could hear four great stags roaring – all real old beasts. It was lovely sitting there watching the autumn sunlight playing on the distant Galloway hills and listening to the sound of stags roaring. (I can still hear them as I write!) Presently in my glasses I found the stalker who had been shooting earlier over the March.

On the other side of me Ken was making good progress. All the time the four stags were roaring and Ken's two dogs were alternately staring in the direction Ken had gone, or searching my face for a word of command to go after him.

Suddenly a hind barked. Ken appeared to be surrounded by hinds, but I thought the big fellow had passed into the next hollow. A shot rang out and I was just in time to see a flurry of antlers as the royal went down. Meanwhile, Ken was running in the other direction and almost at once he had another shot. I could not see another stag, but in fact he had seen the tips of the antlers of the big one going up hill. When the beast came into view he put a bullet through its heart. Even so the great hart went an incredible distance straight up hill. I just caught sight of him as he collapsed and slid down the slope.

Peter and Danny were soon on the scene, and the excited dogs, whom I had released, very soon found the first stag. I joined Ken to help to pull out the big one. He was enormous. When he was put beside the royal, no mean stag, the royal looked but little larger than a Fallow buck! The Great Hart was an eleven-pointer with massive antlers. Danny and these two fine stags, outlined against the gorgeous view right away down the Glen, made a wonderful awe-inspiring picture. It was a marvellous finish to a wonderful day and we did full justice to the huge meal Sallie had prepared for us.

As we carried my suitcases to the car the next day a stag was roaring under the top of Craig Eazle. With the glasses we could pick him out. He had taken over the parcel of hinds that had been with my first stag.

The day after I left, grim tragedy came to the Glen. The face of the Dungeon was dark and scowling, the rock-strewn top shrouded in dense cloud. An aeroplane, piloted by the young laird of a well-known Dumfries estate, was lost in the cloud. It crashed into the rocks at the top of the Dungeon and both occupants were killed – a stern reminder that these wild hills stand aloof from the progress of man; they still belong to the wild red deer, the soaring eagle and the croaking raven.

The following year I was back in the Glen. Ken, John Ransford and myself set off to stalk the Dungeon face, where there was a great hart, an old royal going back. Ken refused to take his rifle. We had not long left the croft when a stag and four hinds rose to their feet behind a large rock. The stag was an uneven eight-pointer, and Ken told John to take him. It was a long shot, and in fact the beast needed a second shot before we were able to perform the last rites. Such an early success, so close to the house, was a surprise.

A long walk brought us to the foot of the Dungeon, where the mass of huge rocks and boulders had tumbled down from the black precipice above. A stag roared on Mullwharchar and suddenly we saw his massive antlers outlined against the sky. He was maybe a mile away and several hundred feet above us on top of a shelf. It was a most impressive sight.

Another stag roared in the corrie in the heart of the Dungeon. Ken picked him up in a moment and gave a gasp of surprise.

'Yon's not the big royal. He's old Cowhorn.'

For six years an enormous stag had come into the area three days before the end of the stag season. He had small brow and bey tines – and no other adornment: just two huge curved 'horns', for all the world like a Highland cow, but much wider. He had had a forty inch span last year. For six years he had outwitted Ken, and I knew he wanted to take this stag more than any he had ever stalked. A hot argument ensued. I refused point blank to go after him. So did John.

The mist was swirling on top of the precipice, and every now and then it curled back like a lace curtain to reveal three hinds right on the skyline. They started to come down. It was a wonderful sight to see these beasts coming down a rock face one would have thought suitable only for goats. Still arguing we covered a good deal of more or less dead ground, with plenty of cover behind huge boulders. Then suddenly there was a great roar. Half way up the corrie was a rock ridge, evidently holding a small basin behind it. The mist swirled about the lip of the ridge, and there, standing on the very edge of the lip, was an enormous stag, his face framed in a huge circle of curved antler. He stood and surveyed the whole glen, and then quietly walked back over the ridge. It seemed that we had only to climb a few hundred feet and then creep to the top of the ridge. But just as we started off a knobber came over the edge of the ridge and lay down in the rocks just below it. From there he could survey every inch of our route.

'Hell!' I said, 'What can we do now, Ken?'

Ken's knowledge of deer is such that he knows exactly how they will react to any set of circumstances.

'There's nae worry about that wee beast,' was Ken's reply.

He took out a white handkerchief and held it motionless, then he had to wave it violently before the knobber got to his feet and ambled over the ridge. I was worried lest he should alert the stag beyond, but Ken explained that the stag would take no notice of this small beast, other than to chase him away. Had it been an old hind it would have been different.

It was not long before we reached the cover of the ridge and, lying down, peeped over. There was a small basin and beyond, about eighty to a hundred yards away, another ridge. In a hollow on the top of this ridge stood another stag – an uneven eight-pointer. There was no sign of old Cowhorn. Just then a great roar came from behind the next ridge. Ken wriggled forward to try to plan out a route for us to cross without alarming the eight-pointer. Suddenly he wriggled backwards tense with excitement. He seized John's rifle (by now John and I had won the argument), crept forward again and fired at once. Old Cowhorn and his hinds had been lying within thirty yards of us immediately under the ridge! It was the old royal that had roared beyond the next ridge. So died old Cowhorn. It wanted only two days to the end of the season, and he had come in only that day! Ken knew where he summered, in a forest twenty miles away as the crow flies. He had an incredible head.

It was not too easy to drag him down the three or four hundred yards of precipitous hillside to where Danny could reach him. We were half way down when John said, 'Look!' There, standing on a rock outlined against the sky, was a wild goat! I have always wanted to shoot a goat, and the goats of this herd were doing damage and had to be shot. Dropping on one knee behind a rock I held steady and squeezed. Head on, he was a 'thin' target as he was a longish shot. At the thud of the bullet he toppled behind the rock – my first Billy!

It was a memorable day. As we followed the deer paths which lead down from the rock faces out across the molinia flows to the good grazing at the burn, there were few happier stalkers in all Scotland.

Incidentally, these very deer paths are of the greatest importance for successful deer control of the future. These great wide areas are being put to their proper use as the ploughs creep up the glen, followed by hundreds of thousands of Sitka spruce transplants. There is no doubt that this land should be forest, and that Sitka spruce is the tree most suited to the ground and one which will bring in the highest profit from these acid peaty areas. But it is very necessary to be able to visualise the deer problem of this huge forest when all has been planted. The deer trails have been on the ground precisely as they are today for many, many centuries. They will be there in precisely the same places long after the present tree crop has been felled. It is essential to take due regard of them when the new plantations are being made! Rides, paths, compartment boundaries and new roads all have to be laid out. It is a simple thing to work some of the main deer trails into this system. Then, when all is in the thicket stage, the deer will pass through on the rides where they can be seen and intercepted. Where the deer trails have been planted up, when all is thicket the deer will still use their old trails, unseen, invisible.

In many areas there is the odd derelict crofter's field, or a corner of better grazing sought after by generations of deer. To leave a few of these unplanted will mean that the stalker in a dense forest will know where to find the deer, and the deer will browse fewer trees!

Another difficulty is the sheep fence between the forest and the unplantable land. In future years, more and more deer will have to be shot on the open land above the forest as the trees close in below. Accesses for the pony through the unbroken fences will be required near the main deer passes. To waste venison on the open hill is unthinkable.

If it is necessary to control deer out of season, because of severe damage, then this distasteful task must be done by an expert who will not destroy indiscriminately first class stags that have taken ten years to produce.

Glen MacArthur

Black is the face of the Dungeon Rocks,
And white is the mist that swirls and mocks.
The drizzle drifts in a steady soak:
The only sound is the Raven's croak,
That and the wee burn's gurgling laugh
As a Red hind stands and licks her calf.

Way down the Glen – a rift in the cloud:
The mist rolls back her unwelcome shroud:
A ray of the sun sweeps over the slope,
In Back Hill of the Bush again there's hope.
Below Craig Eazle brown grass turns gold:
Though Long Loch water stays dark and cold.

Time has stood still in this great wild place:
Man may plant trees that will alter her face.
Long after they've grown and then been cut,
Ravens will croak and the great stags rut,
Passing from Craignaw and Mullwharchar
Under Craig Tarson to feed on Hunt Ha'.

From the Rhinns of the Kells to the dark Wolf's Slock
Eagles will soar whilst the Corbies mock!
Though men may come, and grow old, and go,
The Glen belongs to Red deer and Roe,
While the wee laughing burn runs down to the sea,
Mixed with the water from out of Loch Dee.

XIII

Close Proximity

It is usually the case that when a human being finds himself extremely close to a wild creature, that event has come about more by chance than by skill. Earlier I have recounted how a robin settled four times upon my rifle barrel. I have had a wren settle on my gun barrels when lying in the Solway saltings, waiting for geese. The robin may have sought out human company in the stress of exceptionally hard weather, but the wren never knew he had been near a human being. So, too, dunlin and curlew have walked within a few feet of my hide. Because of the pioneer work done by many bird photographers, it is well accepted that birds will come close to a man well concealed in a hide.

Many animals are more wary than birds, possibly because they cannot escape on the wing. Also they possess an extra faculty – the power to 'wind' their adversary. (Although there is some evidence that some birds – e.g. ducks and perhaps geese – can also scent danger.) At any rate I always find that to be really close to a wild animal is very thrilling.

I was once standing immediately beside a badger path, about twenty yards from the sett. I had watched the well-grown cubs, and the old sow, come out and play and eventually go their different ways. Last of

all the old boar badger came out. He sat and scratched himself and sniffed the air. Then he had another jolly good scratch, obviously enjoying every moment of it. Suddenly he paused in mid-scratch, so to speak, and put up his nose testing the wind. Some freak eddy perhaps brought him a faint puff of my scent from behind, thus cutting off his retreat. He lost his head and came tearing down the path towards me, the sound of his feet resounding on the hollow ground of the sett. In fact his fur brushed against my legs and at the same moment he realised his mistake. Whirling around in a flash, he went pounding back and literally hurtled down the nearest hole. As it happened I had a friend standing behind me who had never seen a badger before that evening. He was quite unnerved, thinking that we had sustained a deliberate attack!

I have twice had an otter swim under my rod, between the reel and my fly in the water. And, of course, it is not uncommon for a hare to come very close to a man, for the silly creature seems to look sideways and backwards, but not always forwards! But, I think, the greatest thrill in Britain is to be exceptionally close to a deer.

When Johnny had learnt to shoot with a twelve-bore, but before he had been trained to use a high-velocity rifle, I gave him permission to try for a doe with S.S.G. I put him about ten paces from a deer path which I was sure would be used by a Fallow doe. I was so intent on impressing upon him that he must shoot only at the neck, and then only if he was absolutely certain of not missing at close range, that I may well have forgotten to make it clear to him which way the deer would come. Up to then he had never been very much nearer than a hundred yards and he did not know a great deal of the habits of deer, although since then he has become a knowledgeable and efficient stalker.

Anyway, he suddenly became aware of a deer standing on the deer path some ten yards from his side. He had not seen it arrive. He was about to raise his gun when the doe barked at him, and he was so unnerved that he nearly fell over backwards. At any rate he never got his gun off!

Once I was stalking down a ditch in a plantation soon after dawn. A yearling Roe buck – not the buck I was after – appeared about twenty yards away. He had a very uneven, poor head and I should have shot him at once, but he started to walk towards me and I decided to wait to see what would happen. He came forward, unconscious of my presence, and stepped onto the mound made from the spoil of the ditch. He followed this until he was standing beside me. I could have dug him in the ribs with my elbow! Instead I just said 'Boo!' He went up about four feet, turning in the air, and tore off. But at fifteen yards he stopped and turned again, standing broadside on, staring at me with incredulous disbelief. Then he went like the wind.

In the dark, deer are sometimes foolish, especially when dazzled by headlights. Once, driving through the forest after dark, with a car load of friends who had been watching deer, I saw two Fallow bucks walking down the road. I accelerated a little to draw nearer before they disappeared. One of the bucks lost his head and ran straight at the car. I had to brake urgently, as did the buck, and he ended up with his nose right over the radiator. On another occasion Bert Smith, one of the New Forest head keepers, was able to lean out of his car window and put his hat on to the antlers of a Fallow buck. I don't know whether it is still wearing his hat!

I have always been very interested in different forms of camouflage. In fact, having seen an excellent Walt Disney film with large oak tree costumes, I wrote to Mr Disney to find out if he would disclose the source from which he obtained them. He did not.

Anyway, on a certain occasion I obtained a green string onion net and, after washing it thoroughly, decided to use it to conceal not only my face, but also the outline of my head and shoulders. Wearing this,

succeeds in breaking off a morsel, then he will turn, kick up his heels, and make three hops. That, to his mind, gives him sufficient privacy to chew in peace. The heel kick is evidently a sign of pleasure.

Now that he has been in the pen for some time it is clear that he has quite a sense of humour. A golden pheasant can run excessively fast for a few yards. Since discovering this, Hoppity takes a grave delight in hopping sedately after the golden pheasants – just to make them run. He will chase any of the ducks and geese in a quiet, inoffensive way. It would seem that a lone rabbit has some need of a playmate.

To return to deer: Japanese Sika stags are immensely powerful. A wounded stag can be dangerous because he will not hesitate to defend himself with all his strength.

I had been after a certain Sika stag on many occasions. Yet very rarely did I get more than a fleeting glimpse of him. Sometimes it would be just his rump disappearing. More often all I saw was a branch moving where he had just been watching me. However, I got to know his territory very well – he spent the day in a dense thicket of young Scots pine.

At last I determined to give up a whole afternoon in order to outwit him. For two hours I waited silently and motionless in a tiny hollow in the more open ground adjoining his lair. Then, with a suddenness that took me by surprise, he let out that wild shrieking whistle which is the mating call of Sika stags. He was only forty yards away, but quite concealed. I waited, tensed, expecting him at any moment. The seconds ticked by into minutes. Nothing happened. After half an hour or so I decided he had gone and made up my mind to seek his slots and see if I could track him. Quietly I stood up and moved a few paces. At once there was another piercing shriek, followed by a queer throaty rumbling. A moment or two later the bushes parted about forty yards away, and out stepped the oldest and most ugly-looking Sika I had ever seen. He had heard my slight movement and thought I was another stag in his territory. With head held low, ready to charge his adversary, making an angry grunting noise, he walked across my front. He carried sharp bayonet-like antlers, with six points. But his flank and heart were masked by bracken so that I could not obtain a clear shot.

Then he paused, turned and started walking straight towards me. I was crouching very low on the ground, wondering when he would spot me and whether he would still regard me as an undesirable intruder and charge, or recognise me as a man and flee. Still he came forward with his head held at such an angle that I could neither put a bullet into his chest nor into his spine above his neck. When he was but ten yards from me he stopped and turned his head slightly sideways to look to one side, thus giving me the first chance I had had since he appeared. He dropped where he stood, stone dead, never having seen me at all.

Some months later I was dining with a doctor near Christchurch. We were talking about deer and presently he said: 'I found an interesting antler last spring.' When he fetched it, much to his surprise, I was able to tell him exactly where he had found it. For without any doubt at all it was a previous year's cast antler from my six-point Sika!

The last story of this book is reprinted by kind permission of the Editor of *The Times*. He had sent down a photographer to record the deer census being taken in the New Forest, so I wrote out the following account of a morning I had spent checking the census:

It is not a question of filling in a form to say that my wife and I were female and male, over the age of twenty-one, and that we had so many lavatories in the house. Taking a deer census is a little more complicated than that.

The census is taken towards the end of March, or in April, when the undergrowth is at its lowest. If it can be left until the spring flush of grass has started, so much the better: after the long winter months of poor feeding, deer then spend longer periods on grazing areas and therefore they are easier to see.

Each keeper in the New Forest has to make a return of the deer on his beat, by the four species, by sexes and, in the case of male deer, by broad age classes. These are divided into two categories, good or poor, and any abnormalities of colour or antler development are also noted. It is from all this information that the shooting plan for the next season is decided.

All this requires a close knowledge of the ground and of the local habits of the deer, combined with patient observation at dawn and dusk often from high seats placed in trees.

There are about thirty white deer in the forest. These are never shot, except when injured, as they give useful information about deer movements and this helps to make the census easier. For instance, a white Fallow buck was the leader of a small herd of nine bucks. One of these was killed by the buckhounds. That left two good six-year-old bucks, two promising bare bucks and three other small bucks (sores and sorels), including one with a broken antler. The white buck was a very good seven-year-old, readily distinguished because his left antler had an abnormal number of 'spellers' – the name given to the small points on top of a Fallow buck's antlers.

After this group had been booked in their various categories, two pieces of information came through which needed checking: the white buck was said to be lame and a group of small bucks, one with a broken antler, had been seen crossing onto an adjoining estate. From this it seemed probable that the small herd of bucks had broken up. As I knew the habits of the white buck fairly well, I decided to go out at dawn to try to check.

I took up my position about eighty yards from a clump of holly bushes on the other side of which were the fields where the white buck was wont to feed. I sat on the ground, with my rifle across my knees in case the buck proved to be badly injured.

The only cover was the skeleton of a holly bush which had been burnt in a fire the year before, and a few bracken fronds grown last summer through the dead branches of the holly.

In contrast to the knife-edged north-easterly winds which had seared the forest for the past ten days, the morning was mild and moist. The earth smelt fresh: full of the promise of spring. With delight I heard a curlew making his liquid, bubbling spring call. He was the first to return to the breeding ground. Peewits wheeled, crying plaintively, their wings beating the air loudly as they turned. One settled on the close-cropped turf only fifteen yards away, and it was a full minute before he saw me. In the distance a snipe called: 'Chip-er, chip-er, chip-er'. I could not see him, but I knew he was flying over the bog below the road.

Suddenly I saw the hind-quarters of a white deer between two holly bushes and presently a white buck stepped forward into the open. As he looked over his shoulder, staring into the holly bushes, I could see that his left antler carried the fine array of spellers; the palms were broad and his span wide. He was the same buck.

I studied him carefully through powerful field-glasses. He was in poor condition; ten days of biting winds and shrivelled food had not been conducive to weight building. Yet he was perfectly sound.

I could now see the antlers of three more bucks behind him. Soon they too stepped into the open – three great bucks, two with huge antlers, making even the white buck look small, and the third only slightly inferior. The white buck had indeed changed his company. They were all uneasy about something in the holly bushes.

Then, with mincing steps and head held high, the white buck started to follow a deer path across the heather. Unhurried, and seemingly without a care in the world, the three great bucks followed.

It was now obvious that their route would bring them very close to where I was sitting. Although the wind was in my favour I expected them to become aware of me when they reached a point some twenty yards away, for I was not well concealed. However, the white buck never paused; he walked steadily forward, coming nearer and nearer. It was intensely exciting. Soon he was closer than I had ever been to a Fallow buck; for an old Fallow buck is one of the most wary and alert animals of all.

Suddenly he came round the holly stump to find himself face to face with me at no distance at all. He threw up his head and his front legs went rigid, his cleaves spread wide open, cutting deeply into the ground. Then he threw himself backwards, turning so rapidly that the eye could scarcely take in the movement.

I have often noticed that when, by chance, a wild animal comes very close to a man, it seems as though its mind cannot accept what its eyes tell it, especially if it has not winded danger. So it was now. After rushing wildly for some ten yards, the white buck turned to stare in wonder at me. He stood, broadside on, stock still, for all the world like a statue of white marble. Beyond him were the three great bucks, standing equally motionless, their great antlers held high, immobile, as if carved out of oak. They had not seen me. In fact they never knew what was the danger. Then the muscles of the white buck's haunch rippled and his legs flexed slightly. With a great bound he was away, followed immediately by the three great bucks.

In a few moments they were running the skyline of the hill, clear-cut like clockwork toys, each spaced an exact distance from the next. It was difficult to believe that so short a time before they had been so close. I stood up and measured the distance between the slots, where the white buck had stopped, and the bag upon which I had sat. It was exactly seven feet! It isn't really necessary to get quite so close in order to take a census.

Fawn, Pricket, Sorrel, Sore,
Bare Buck and Buck

Today I stood beside a tiny fawn:
Beauty and innocence so newly born.

Dappled shadow, sleeping beneath the fern,
Born yesterday.
The world is yours: and yet you've all to learn.
Go, run and play
Before you find that life is harsh and stern.

Seek out the woodland paths and winding burn:
Go where you may.
Hold still and watch – experience you'll earn.
And then, one day,
Antlers held high, a Great Buck, you'll return.

Bibliography

The following are some of the many good deer books which are of general interest to those who watch, study and manage deer. For the forester, Richard Prior's *Trees and Deer* is a necessity.

Clutton-Brock, Guiness and Alton, *Red Deer Behaviour and Ecology*, Edinburgh University Press, 1982.

Darling, Fraser, *A Herd of Red Deer*, Oxford University Press, London, 1937.

de Nahlik, A. J., *Wild Deer, Culling, Conservation and Management*, Ashford Press, Southampton, 1987.

Harris, Roy A. and Duff, K. R., *Wild Deer in Britain*, David & Charles, Newton Abbot, 1970.

Hart-Davis, Duff, *Monarchs of the Glen*, Jonathan Cape, London, 1978.

Hingston, Frederick, *Deer Parks and Deer of Great Britain*, Barracuda, Buckingham, 1988.

Holmes, Frank, *Following the Roe*, Bartholomew, Edinburgh, 1974.

Lascelles, Hon. G., *Thirty-five Years in the New Forest*, Edward Arnold, London, 1915.

Luxmoore, Edmund, *Deer Stalking*, David & Charles, Newton Abbot, 1980.

Millais, J. G., *British Deer and their Horns*, Henry Sotheran, London, 1897.

Page, F. J. Taylor (ed.), *Field Guide to British Deer*, Blackwell, Oxford, 1982.

Perry, Richard, *The Watcher and the Red Deer*, David & Charles, Newton Abbot, 1952.

Prior, Richard, *Trees and Deer*, Batsford, London, 1983.
Modern Roe Stalking, Tideline, Rhyl, 1985.

Tegner, Henry, *The Tale of the Deer Forest*, 1957.

Whitehead, Kenneth, *Hunting and Stalking Deer in Great Britain through the Ages*, Batsford, London, 1980.

The Deer of Great Britain and Ireland, Routledge, London, 1964.

Practical Deer Stalking, Constable, London, 1986.

I must also mention Robin Page's *The Fox and the Orchid* (Quiller Press, 1982). This excellent book should be on every countryman's bookshelf, for it puts all country sport (including a chapter on deer) into proper perspective.